# {Let Me Tell You What Your Teens Are Telling Me}

by Blaine Bartel

**Harrison House**
Tulsa, Oklahoma

# Contents

>>

The thing that impresses
me most about America
is the way parents
obey their children.

Edward VIII, King of England

# Preface >>

A couple of years ago a well-respected traveling teacher/evangelist who travels all over America asked me, "Blaine, in all of your experience with young people, what would you say are the top two problems with American teenagers?"

The answer came right out before I realized what I was saying. I said, "Dad and Mom."

If you are parenting teenagers right now or are a leader in a youth group, this book will be the wisdom you need to not only get through it but also to help you be that godly influence in your kids' lives. We are going to look at what the Bible says with regard to authority, growing up, and developing a teenager's life to love and serve God.

Do you know what your teenager is thinking? Do you understand why they do the things they do and say the things they say? If you are the parent of a teenager, and especially if you are a parent of more than one teenager, you need help!

If you are not a parent of a teenager, you will still deal with teenagers in your life. They may be your friends' kids or your neighbor's kids or your sisters' and brothers' kids. Or maybe you have grandchildren who are teenagers. And what you are going to find is that in these troubled times, there are a lot of troubled teenagers.

Some of these troubled young people are rebelling against their parents, and your influence could bring them around. Some are not being parented by anyone, and your influence could make the difference in their lives. And if some are in your own home, you may be confused and don't have the foggiest idea what to do with them! Whatever your contact with teenagers, I believe this book will help you.

> >

**The important thing to remember is that we are not just raising our kids so that they don't embarrass us! We are training up the next generation of citizens for our nations—and more significantly for the kingdom of God.**

As Cathy and I have grown up as parents—and we've really worked at parenting—we have found that when our kids are messing up or doing something they shouldn't be doing, it usually comes back to us. In most cases we will look at each other and say, "You know what? We need to correct some things that we're doing here, make some adjustments ourselves, and then change some guidelines for the kids."

Through years of studying what happens in teenagers' lives and having had the chance to counsel so many, I have found that whatever the problem is, it usually goes right back to Mom and Dad. Of course, there are other factors that are involved with young people. They can be greatly influenced by friends and teachers and even celebrities. But how teenagers live their lives really comes down to their family and how their parents are raising them.

If you are parenting a teenager, I know this book will help you! If you have teenagers in your life, these biblical principles can also help you to be a good, godly influence in their lives. The important thing to remember is that we are not just raising our kids so that they don't embarrass us! We are training up the next generation of citizens for our nations—and more significantly for the kingdom of God.

Teenagers today are the leaders of tomorrow. And for our future to be bright, our kids must love God and have a passion to serve Him with their whole heart, soul, mind, and strength. For that to happen, we need God's wisdom!

# 3 Things That Won't Make Your Teen Happy[1]

1.    Worldly fame.

2.    Romantic love.

3.    Much money.

{
Blessed *is* every one who fears the LORD,
Who walks in His ways.
When you eat the labor of your hands,
You *shall be* happy, and *it shall be* well with you.
}

Psalm 128:1,2

>>

# Having children makes you no more a parent than having a piano makes you a pianist.

Michael Levine

One

# Confessions of a Former Parenting Expert

W hen I started in ministry, I was a youth pastor. Being around twenty years old, I made a habit of telling parents of teenagers how to raise their kids. Because I was a youth pastor and knew so many young people as well as I did, I thought for sure that I had it all figured out. But as my own kids started going through the teenage years, I realized that I wasn't as smart as I thought I was. I am no longer the cocky youth pastor who knew exactly how to do this and had an instant solution for every problem. I am now a member of the "Reality Parenting Club."

## Reality Parenting

I learn something new every day about raising teenagers. I am continuously humbled by the fact that in order to be successful, we must have guidance from God and His Word. At the end of the day when our kids are all home and safely asleep in their beds, thank God! He helped us through another day. And when I don't have a clue and can't seem to make myself clear to them, I know we can count on the Lord to strengthen and assist us in this monumental task.

Most important, I cannot read enough of God's Word and other books on parenting to keep our kids and other kids straight (and to keep me sane). I need wisdom!

> If any of you lacks wisdom, let him ask of God, who gives to all liberally and without reproach, and it will be given to him.
>
> James 1:5

In this process of raising our teenagers, we find out very quickly that there is no three-step process or seven-point formula that will answer every question and solve every problem. The Word of God gives us principles and guidelines, but we have to be led by the Holy Spirit in the details. And the details can get pretty messy and complicated at times! There is no cookie-cutter recipe for raising a teenager that will insure you that they will turn out to be a perfect adult. You just follow God's Word, pray, believe, and have faith in God to see you and your kids through it.

Parenting requires a nonstop, deep-in-the-trenches commitment. This means asking questions—and then listening carefully and prayerfully to the answers. It means repeating answers to their questions—often. And then there's the probing, investigating, praying, analyzing, and critiquing. And by the way, all of this can happen in one hour of one day and several times during the day!

Cathy and I have discovered that all teenagers are not created equal. They're all different. It would be great if God just made them all the same. There would be one kind of teenager, and once you figured out one, you would simply apply everything you knew to all the others in your life. But God didn't do that. One teenager can be so different from the next, even in the same family. We have three and they are completely unique individuals.

Our oldest is Jeremy. He is thoughtful, deliberate, artistic, quiet—and determined. Dillon is our middle son, and he is creative, musical, outgoing, and what we call "lawyerly." That means he likes to argue his case from time to time. Brock, our youngest, is extremely competitive and can even be compulsive. He has kept every one of his toy cars from when he was a little boy, they are all organized carefully on his

> >

**Reality parenting is an adventure! Like anything else in life, you can either determine to trust God and find the joy in it or rely on yourself and hate every minute of it.**

dresser, and there are hundreds of them! They are arranged a certain way and they have to stay that way.

Again, there are principles from God's Word that work for all of our teenagers, but there are different styles and methods that you have to find to work these principles with each kid. Just when you think you have something figured out, one of the other kids does something completely different, and you have to start all over again in teaching and implementing that principle or truth.

Reality parenting is an adventure! Like anything else in life, you can either determine to trust God and find the joy in it or rely on yourself and hate every minute of it. In my experience, trusting God is the only way to get through it. He understands our kids better than we do, and He can clue us in on what's going on with them and how we should deal with them.

## Identify

One of the things God has shown me is that we forget what it was like when we were teenagers. We forget to identify with where our kids are in growing up and what that is like. Along with that, we often don't listen to them and ask God to give us wisdom about who they are and what they're trying to tell us about themselves. Not understanding them—either because we're not trying to or just don't get it—can really frustrate them. We have to look, listen, and remember how we felt when we were their age.

We forget what it was like to be a teenager. But did you know that God gave us the ability to identify with others—even teenagers? He exhorts us in His Word to understand where they are and what they are going through. Then we can instruct them and discipline them with love and compassion instead of getting bent out of shape every time something goes wrong with them. We can reach them if we make that effort to identify with them and really get into their world. Here is what the apostle Paul wrote about this.

> > >

Even though I am free of the demands and expectations of everyone, I have voluntarily become a servant to any and all in order to reach a wide range of people.

1 Corinthians 9:19 MESSAGE

**There is nothing more staggering and attention getting to a teenager than an adult who "gets them," who knows their language and understands what they are thinking, feeling, and experiencing.**

I used *The Message* translation so that you could really catch the spirit of what the apostle Paul was saying to the church at Corinth. This was a church that was like modern-day Los Angeles. Being a port city, Corinth was a mosaic of different people groups, and worldwide commerce abounded there. There were all kinds of cultures and religions in the city. Paul was trying to help the believers relate to each other in a biblical manner and also to find a way to effectively convey the gospel to the diverse people groups in their city. He went on to describe these people and how he dealt with them.

> ...religious, nonreligious, meticulous moralists, loose-living immoralists, the defeated, the demoralized—whoever. I didn't take on their way of life. I kept my bearings in Christ—but I entered their world and tried to experience things from their point of view. I've become just about every sort of servant there is in my attempts to lead those I meet into a God-saved life. I did all of this because of the Message. I didn't want to just talk about it; I wanted to be *in* on it!
>
> 1 Corinthians 9:20-23 MESSAGE

Paul tells the Corinthians that he will serve people in any way to bring them the truth of the gospel. He exhorts them not only to preach and teach, but to preach and teach with some understanding of the people they are ministering to. We are to step into their shoes. Look at life through their eyes. Discern their needs and concerns. Identify with them—then preach and teach the gospel in a way they can understand it and receive it.

This is a great principle for dealing with teenagers! We must understand where they are coming from so we can be effective in giving them instruction, disciplining them, and influencing them to obey God's Word and follow His Spirit. There is nothing more staggering and attention getting to a teenager than an adult who "gets them," who knows their language and understands what they are thinking, feeling, and experiencing.

## Run To Win

As a green, wet-behind-the-ears youth pastor, I had no idea how much perseverance it took to raise a teenager. In this same passage in 1 Corinthians, Paul expresses his passion to reach the lost no matter what it cost him personally. I have discovered that you have to have that same passion to parent a teenager!

You've all been to the stadium and seen the athletes race. Everyone runs; one wins. Run to win. All good athletes train hard. They do it for a gold medal that tarnishes and fades. You're after one that's gold eternally.

I don't know about you, but I'm running hard for the finish line. I'm giving it everything I've got. No sloppy living for me! I'm staying alert and in top condition. I'm not going to get caught napping, telling everyone else all about it and then missing out myself.

1 Corinthians 9:24-27 MESSAGE

> >

One of the main things I have learned through the years is that young people have a culture all their own. They are like a tribe within America. They have their own tribal music. They have their own tribal language. They have their tribal huts—their bedrooms! They have tribal meeting places, which can be everything from a convenience store parking lot to a church youth center. And like our Native American tribes, they have clans within their tribe, especially in school.

Read this passage again in the context of reaching your kids. Paul says, "Man, we got to go for it. We can't just be in the race of parenting. We can't make a half-hearted attempt to parent just to get through the years until we get our kids out the door." Paul said that we need to run to win. Then he told us how to win.

## Keep Yourself in Shape

To win, we have to be like an athlete training for the Olympics. We have to work hard, train hard, and stay fit ourselves. We have to keep our own lives right with God because how we live our lives before our kids will have more impact on them than anything we say to them. We can't really expect them to love God, read and study His Word, pray, and live by the Spirit if we are out living for ourselves and doing what is right in our own eyes. We must model the Christian life for them—and that includes admitting we are wrong when we mess up, repenting to God, setting things right, and continuing to move forward in Him. Being a good Christian example does not mean you do everything perfectly; it just means doing the best you can in following Jesus Christ in all honesty.

## Get God's Strategy

To win, we also have to strategize. Just like an athlete will figure out how to win each race, we have to be prayerful, thoughtful, and deliberate when we deal with our teenagers. Athletes don't just show up and run. They consider who they are running against, the challenges of the course they are running that day, and even what the crowd will be like as they run. They take the time to carefully and prayerfully consider all the facts and information they are given and then choose the best strategy possible in order to win.

As Christians, we have the advantage of knowing God, and He knows everything. He knows our kids better than we do, and sometimes only the Holy Spirit can tell us what's going on with them. He knows the challenges and attacks that will come against them. And even if we don't heed His warnings and are hit by the enemy, we can go to Him and get His plan to overcome and defeat the enemy. Once we have God's Word and the Holy Spirit's revelation of what we are dealing with and how to deal with it—which is His strategy—then we know we can win.

Does this sound like a lot of work to you? Sometimes it is, but your kids are worth it! Paul was saying that reaching people with the gospel doesn't come naturally and without preparation, and neither does parenting. It won't come to you on the fly. You must pray and seek God's wisdom and leading with regard to your kids. You must study and learn from others, and you must persevere. Believe me, your kids will notice when you don't give up on them. It means everything to them that no matter what they do you are still there, giving them all you've got. They may not thank you for it now, but one day they will!

## A Tribe of Their Own

One of the main things I have learned through the years is that young people have a culture all their own. They are like a tribe within America. They have their own tribal music. They have their own tribal language. They have their tribal huts—their bedrooms! They have tribal meeting places, which can be everything from a convenience store parking lot to a church youth center. And like our Native American tribes, they have clans within their tribe, especially in school. They have the nerd clan, the jock clan, the intellectual clan, the preppy clan, the gang clan, the druggie clan, the gothic clan, and—thank God—many schools now have the Jesus clan.

To figure out how to get into their world and reach them, to keep them firmly rooted and grounded in God, we need to understand the culture of their tribe and what clan or clans they gravitate toward. As a parent of teenagers, I find this concept very comforting. My kids are part of a foreign tribe, and I need to approach them in the same way I would approach a tribe in Africa or New Guinea!

It means a lot to kids when someone tries to see something from their point of view, but the same is true for adults. You know how much it means to you when your boss takes a moment to come in and talk to you about your job. He asks you, "What's going on? Is there a way that I can help you to do your job better or make it easier for you?" It's great when somebody takes time to consider what's going on in your world.

Wives love it when their husbands sit down and take the time to ask, "Honey, what's going on in your life right now? How can I help you? What's going on at home with the kids?" or, "What's going on at your office?" Everyone appreciates it when somebody tries to jump into their world, see life from their point of view, and try to help them and encourage them.

The same thing is true for teenagers. Parents who take time to understand and listen to their kids will have far better results in keeping them on their mission for Christ as they grow up. Taking time may mean talking to your kids when you pick them up from school instead of listening to a CD, the radio, or talking on your cell phone. It may mean getting up a little earlier to make certain you have breakfast together. And then there may be times when you plan special vacations or getaways just so you can spend time together.

This kind of attention is what your kids really want. If you don't give them this kind of attention—if you don't make the effort to enter and understand their world and then include them in yours from time to time—then you will find them getting your attention in negative and destructive ways. This is why it is so important for you to stay in touch with your teenagers and keep up-to-date on what's going on in their lives. Again, they may call you a pest and even tell you you're intruding on their privacy, but one day they will thank you for caring enough to ask questions.

You have to get a grip on the reality of parenting teenagers. It's not easy! But if you pay the price with your time and effort early in their lives, you won't be like so many parents who pay a terrible price at the end of their child's teenage years. Kids who are allowed to run free without any guidance and instruction will cost their parents much more time, money, and heartache in the end than would have been required from the beginning. Run the race of parenting in order to win. And realize that they are growing up in a time and place, in circumstances and with people, which you never experienced when you were growing up.

If you treat your teenagers with respect and show compassion and understanding for the challenges they are facing, they are far more likely to let you into their life and influence them. So I am going to help you out by telling you the things that they are telling me. If you know what is going on in their heads and hearts, you stand a better chance of not only living through the experience of raising teenagers, but also helping them fulfill the plan of God for their lives with joy.

# 3 Things That Will Make Your Teen Brilliant[1]

Just because your teenager has a brain doesn't mean they are using it all that much. If they learn to be a life-long learner they will go far in life. Here are three qualities that will make them a great learner.

1.  Teach them to ask questions. Science is simply the art of asking lots of questions and searching for the answer. What questions are they asking? Encourage them to ask lots of questions when they are around people who know more than they do.

2.  Help them develop a teachable spirit. Someone once said, "It's what you learn after you know it all that counts." Help them make a habit of never going to sleep without having learned something new that day.

3. Challenge them to have passion. One time a student of philosophy asked his teacher how he could become a man of great wisdom. The teacher said, "Follow me and I will show you." The teacher waded into the ocean and the student followed him. The wise teacher then held his young pupil under water until the student began to kick and fight his way to the surface. The student, gasping for air, asked, "What did you do that for?" The wise teacher replied, "When you want wisdom as much as you wanted air, you will find it."

>>

# Children today are tyrants. They contradict their parents, gobble their food, and tyrannize their teachers.

Socrates (470-399 B.C.)

Two

# "I'm a little brain-damaged, so get used to it."

A young person at Oneighty a number of months ago was walking around with this black t-shirt on. It had great big words on the back that said, "Never underestimate the power of stupid people in large groups!" That's so true! You get two or more teenagers together and you never know what's going to happen or what they are going to do.

Actually, teenagers don't usually say that they're brain damaged. What they say is, "I'm a teenager. What do you expect? Of course I do this kind of stuff!" or "I wasn't thinking! I don't know why I did that." And if you look back at your teenage years, you will probably find times when you thought the same thing. Just think about some of the crazy things that you did when you were a young person. You know you did crazy stuff! You did things that you would never do today. Why? Because back then you were brain-damaged as well.

I almost hate to share this, but it illustrates what I'm talking about. When I was a teenager my buddy and I were on a school bus coming home from school. We were at the back of the bus, looking out the window, and saw another school bus with a bunch of our friends on it traveling behind us. At that moment our brains told us that the best thing to do would be to pull down our pants and moon them.

We were caught, of course, and suspended from school for three days. My parents went even further and grounded me. I remember telling my Mom and Dad, "I don't know why I did that. I just did it, you know?" To this day, I don't know why I did this!

If you're not sure that teenagers do stupid things, I have proof. I have pictures of brain-damaged teenagers doing many crazy things. One is of a kid who is roller-blading on his father's greenhouse. Another shows a teenager skateboarding off the top of a building.

> >

**God knows that young people are prone to foolishness and fads, and the Bible says that the cure for this is tough-minded discipline.**

One shows a teenager going street canoeing, and another is performing a balcony free-fall. They just don't think!

## God Knows

In case you are thinking that what I'm saying is unscriptural, let me give you some verses to meditate on.

> The glory of young men is their strength, and the beauty of old men is their gray head [suggesting wisdom and experience].
>
> Proverbs 20:29 AMP

This is saying that when you get older you get smarter. You have acquired some wisdom. You have gained some experience. You have learned why you should do things or why you shouldn't do things. When you are young you have a lot of energy, but unfortunately you don't always have the wisdom and understanding to go with it.

> Foolishness is bound up in the heart of a child, but the rod of discipline will drive it far from him.
>
> Proverbs 22:15

God knows that young people are prone to foolishness and fads, and the Bible says that the cure for this

21

is tough-minded discipline. God tells us in this verse in Proverbs just what the problem is with young people. They're going to be prone to foolish acts, crazy thinking, and fads of their culture. They are going to say and do things that are completely irrational and illogical simply because their peers are doing it or it seemed right to them at the time.

Praise God, He also tells us the answer to this problem. There is a medicine to cure this disease! He lets us know that we can bring teenagers to sanity and build godly character in them if we discipline them. He promises that when they experience some form of pain or discomfort because of their foolish words or actions, and we take them to the Word of God and show them that what they said or did opposed God's will for their lives, it will drive foolishness out of their lives.

Just how does this work? When your teenager does something stupid, you discipline them so that they remember that doing that stupid thing did not give them the pleasure they thought they'd get. In fact, it brought displeasure. In my case, my parents grounded me for a pretty good period of time. Instead of continuing to have fun with my friends, I stayed home and was deprived of fun.

To further make your point, when your kids do something good, you reward them. Take them on a fun weekend trip with a couple of their friends or give them something they've been believing God for. After a while of suffering pain or displeasure when they mess up and getting rewarded when they stay on track with God, they will want to do the right thing and think before they say or do something.

This is the point of disciplining a teenager—to train them to think and pray and consider God's Word before they speak or act. (To be honest, we need a lot more adults in the church who do this!)

I can tell you from personal experience that there is nothing like disciplining your teenager, who has been rebellious or just plain stupid, and seeing the eyes of their understanding enlightened! When they fully recognize how they have been thinking, speaking, and acting contrary to God's Word and experience the consequences

> >

**Teenagers do stupid things, and parents need to understand that. If they do, when something crazy happens, they won't completely lose it and go ballistic every time. They will just learn to deal with it.**

of their actions, their lives are changed. It may take a time or two, but eventually they will see the light.

## Science Knows

Science always discovers what God has already told us in His Word, and teenagers are no exception. I came across an article on the Internet titled "Why Teenagers are Weird." In the story they document some studies that were done on the adolescent brain. I won't go into all the research on this, but it helps us understand what our kids are thinking and why they do the things they do.

There are two major development spurts when the young brain develops and grows. The first is in the womb. They say that much of the brain's development occurs before birth. When the baby is in the womb the brain grows like crazy. By the time the child is six years old, 90-95 percent of the brain's development has taken place. Then it is relatively dormant for years.

The last 5 percent of the development of the brain happens during adolescence. This is when the next major growth spurt happens. So your teenager is in a tremendous stage of brain development, which explains a lot of their hair-brained thinking and activity. While their brain is growing and the world is expanding, they are trying to figure out how to deal with it.

Here is a quote from the article.

> By age six, a child's brain has already achieved 95 percent of its adult structure. Research—much of it based on brain scans of infants—shows that neutron connections form at a dizzying speed during the period from birth to three. Brand new

research has uncovered a second period of rapid brain development stretching from preadolescence through to the early twenties. The brain is undergoing more change now than in any other time, accept just after birth.

Linda Spear, Professor of Psychology
Binghamton University, New York

New connections throughout the adolescent brain are being made during the teenage years. This includes the gray matter where we do our rational thinking. Therefore, rationality is being further developed in youth.

The brain is feverishly reshaping itself—pruning neutral connections at the rate of thirty thousand per second, producing a leaner, meaner brain. The biggest changes are occurring in the brain's prefrontal cortex, located right behind the forehead, which governs executive thinking or ability to use logic, make sound decisions, size up potential risks…

Knowing that this decision-making area is still under construction explains plenty about teenagers. Researchers have found that, even in those who generally show good judgment, the quality of decision making fizzles in moments of high arousal emotion—whether happiness, anger, or jealousy— particularly when teens are with their peers. It overrides logic. Even the smart ones momentarily become dumb.

This phenomenon may help to explain why one teen starts smoking even though he or she knows it will hurt their track time. Or another shoplifts a pack of gum while they have $5 in their pocket.

Linda Spear, Professor of Psychology
Binghamton University, New York[1]

What this boils down to is that science has again discovered what God knew from the beginning and wrote in His Word, that young people are prone to foolishness.

## Now You Know, So What Are You Going to Do About It?

Teenagers do stupid things, and parents need to understand that. If they do, when something crazy happens, they won't completely lose it and go ballistic every time. They will just learn to deal with it. If they don't understand and accept this fact, then they will probably throw a wild fit every time their kids say or do something crazy. They won't deal with it, and their teenagers will never learn to think before they act or seek the wisdom of God in all they say and do. Parents must deal with their kids' "brain-damaged" behavior as they are growing up. There is nothing worse than an adult who still acts brain-damaged!

Let me warn you. It's going to take time after time after time of explaining and disciplining. They rarely catch on the first time. You're going to have to work continually at putting godly wisdom and knowledge—the

> >

Remember that the brain damage is temporary! It is not going to last forever. This is your hope and one of the greatest things that you can hold on to. There's a day coming when they are going to figure it out. They're going to be all right. So all you have to do is keep walking in God's wisdom, praying, disciplining, instructing, and believing His Word until they pass through this season of insanity.

right stuff—into their heads. They need lots of help connecting the dots and figuring out how things work.

Following are some things that you can do to help make the process a little easier.

## Stop the Shock

What does that mean? Quit having emotional outbursts of shock and dismay every time they say or do something you never could have anticipated. Don't act so surprised that your teenagers do stupid, crazy things. Learn to deal confidently and calmly with stupidity. Just say, "Hey, I understand. But we're going to make sure this doesn't happen again. Let's sit down and work this through. We'll figure this out together. I'll help you to see how you can avoid making this decision again."

## Thrills and Chills

Most teenagers crave excitement. They want to do things that are exciting and adventurous. You can see to it that they have extracurricular activities in school that challenge them and cause them to stay focused but also give them a rush of excitement. If you don't step in and monitor your kids' activities, they will probably find things to do that will harm themselves.

Many teenagers want to be at risk. They want to try new things. They want to get out there and experiment with their world. This is the youth pastor's main job, right? To find ways of providing that outlet for our young people while teaching them about God. But parents also have to help them find safe risks, opportunities to have a good time without killing themselves.

All kinds of sports fall under this category, even things like skiing, snowboarding, rock climbing, or trampolining. Maybe they find adventure in Boy Scouts or going to camp in the summers. Just find things that they can do and like to do that provide a thrill and a chill but will not put them in harm's way too much.

## Watch the Time

Did you know that 40 percent of a teenager's time is discretionary? In other words, they figure out what to do with it. During nearly half of their day, they decide what they're going to do. If you give a young person that much time to figure out what they're going to do, they will usually find their way into trouble!

We've got to get involved and bring specific activities into that free time. I'm not saying that they can never have some time to rest, relax, read, watch television, or play computer games. But we've got to keep them busy. We've got to find things for them to get involved with, extracurricular activities or hobbies that they enjoy. We've also got to involve them in household chores and maintenance. They need to understand that being a part of a family means doing their part, and it also builds their self-esteem to be trusted with certain responsibilities.

Studies show that kids who are involved in supervised activities from one to four hours a week are 49 percent less likely to use drugs and 37 percent less likely to become a teen parent. So it is important for parents to monitor a teenager's time and make sure they are busy doing the right things.

## Your Greatest Hope

Remember that the brain damage is temporary! It is not going to last forever. This is your hope and one of the greatest things that you can hold on to. There's a day coming when they are going to figure it out. They're going to be all right. So all you have to do is keep walking in God's wisdom, praying, disciplining, instructing, and believing His Word until they pass through this season of insanity.

You can pass along this hope to your teenagers too. Every now and then, it's a good idea to let them know that there will come a day when they won't feel and act quite so crazy as they are feeling and acting now. You will be there to help them keep it together, and eventually they are going to come through it. After that, they will still mess up from time to time—as all human beings do—but they won't be quite so hair-brained as they are now!

# 4 Things Your Teen Should Look for in a Mentor[2]

A mentor is critical in the life of every successful person. Joshua had Moses. Elisha had Elijah. The disciples had Jesus. Oftentimes, mentors won't seek you out—we have to find them. Here are 4 clues in helping your teenager find the right one for them.

1. A good track record. Look for someone who has a good history of success in the thing they want to do.

2. Mutual benefit. Every great relationship will be good for both people. It is never one-sided. What can they do to help this potential mentor, bringing benefit to them?

3. Unforced relationship. Allow the mentoring relationship to develop naturally. Don't try to force someone into this. Just find a way to be around this person by serving, helping, and contributing any way they can.

4. Ask the right questions at the right time. Don't overwhelm this person to the point they want to avoid you. Be sensitive to the right opportunities to learn. Most of the time, they'll learn more by observing them.

\>\>

**C**hildren are natural
mimics who act like their parents
despite every effort to teach
them good manners.

Anonymous

Three

# "Quit trying to act perfect because it's obvious that you're not."

I find a lot of young people believe that their parents are hypocrites—not because they make mistakes, but because they try to cover them up or they deny they made a mistake in the first place. Life is about learning from our mistakes and the mistakes of others, and if we go through life faking it, never acknowledging our faults and failures or doing anything about them, so will our kids.

One of the things our kids need to see is that we know how to make adjustments as parents; that when we miss it, we own it, repent of it, make things right, and keep going. By repent, I don't mean to just say, "Oh my, I'm sorry. I guess I made a mistake." What I mean is that we say, "That was wrong, and I'm changing my thinking and my behavior." When our kids see us change our way of thinking and behavior so that we line up with God's Word, they will have no argument with us when we discipline them to do the same.

Your kids watch how you deal with your problems and sins. It's good for them to see you persevere to change a bad habit or battle to overcome a fault in your life. If you live that way, they won't have a problem with your making a mistake from time to time, especially when it comes to making decisions with regard to them. They simply want to see you have real humility. They want to see you admit you were wrong and make it right. They can respect you for that, and it gives them a model they can follow.

> >

**The two greatest words I believe you can share with your teenager are: forgive me.**

When kids see you deal righteously with your sins and faults, they have hope that if they mess up in the future, it's not the end of the world. God still loves them and forgives them. You still love them and forgive them. And they can admit it, repent, and go on without feeling ashamed and destroyed. Moreover, when they have this godly model to follow, they will not be easily tempted to become rebellious and contentious every time you or they mess up. Instead, they will know what to do to make things right again.

Think back on your life. Who were the people that you really looked up to and respected? Maybe they were your parents or a friend of your parents, an employer, a Sunday school teacher or pastor, a sports coach, a music instructor, a schoolteacher, or even a television character. This person always seemed to make the right decisions and everyone around them was so happy all the time. But what happened when that person made a mistake? Didn't that make you feel better?

When you saw that the person you admired and respected wasn't perfect and actually made a bad decision now and then, didn't it give you hope? After all, if that person messed up and admitted it, got some things straight, and then went on with their life, then you could do the same thing. You thought to yourself, *I guess even the best people make mistakes. We all have to deal with not being perfect. So I can do the same. Messing up is not the end of the world, and I'm going to be okay if I just stick with God.*

## Forgive Me

Humility is what our kids need to see, and the two greatest words I believe you can share with your teenager are: forgive me. If you've never said those words to your teenager, they probably need to hear them. No parent is perfect, and you have probably failed them or let them down a time or two.

I'll never forget the day Cathy and the kids and I were on our way to church in our first brand-new van. It was beautiful and I was so proud of it. So I made the decision that all good fathers make when you get a new vehicle. There would be no food and drink in it. Of course, we had always eaten and drank in our previous vehicles, but this was different. This was our new van, which required a new rule because I was determined to keep our new van spotlessly clean. For the rest of eternity it would look just like it did when it came out of the showroom at the dealership.

On the first Sunday after getting our new van, we were rushing around, running late, and hadn't had time to drink our coffee. Cathy asked me if she could please bring her coffee into the nice, new van. Being a great, understanding husband, I said yes. But I told her, "Do not spill the coffee."

We got in the van and—being late—I quickly put it in reverse. I wasn't used to a new car in which the transmission actually worked, where it didn't take a second or two to slowly creep into gear. Thus, the moment I hit reverse, the van immediately jerked back. Of course, Cathy's coffee went flying all over the van. It was on the carpet, on the seats, and everywhere!

What was my response? I lost it! I mean, I was mad! After all, I had just told her not to spill her coffee. She knew what I had requested and did it anyway! This wasn't my fault! She should have been more careful. So all the way to church I was puffing and wheezing and snorting, making it obvious that I was very displeased and upset.

When we got to church I got out of the van and slammed the door. Then I marched to the church building, seething inside. When we reached the doors, I was confronted with those wonderful Church on the Move greeters. They were just as friendly as could be. "Hey, Pastor Blaine! How are you doing?"

Without hesitation, I smiled my church smile and said, "Fine! Thank you. Praise God! Amen." I was still angry with Cathy, and our kids were dragging along behind us. They all had a front row seat to watch Dad be a jerk until they escaped into their classes.

My heart was still hard as a rock when Cathy and I entered the adult service. Praise and worship music began, and I automatically got right into it. I was singing, "Hallelujah!" But it was all sticking in my throat. It was hard to praise God out of a pure heart when I was so ticked at Cathy, and now she was ticked at me. By the time I raised my hands just a little bit, she turned to me with a look that said, "You hypocrite."

> >

**If your kids hear you say, "Forgive me"—especially if the person you wronged was them—they will be more likely to not be stubborn and unrepentant when you confront them with their own sins and mistakes.**

Finally I couldn't stand it anymore. I grabbed her hand and asked her to forgive me. I knew better than to come to worship God before making it right with someone I had offended. Jesus' words were ringing in my ears.

> Therefore if you bring your gift to the altar, and there remember that your brother has something against you, leave your gift there before the altar, and go your way. First be reconciled to your brother, and then come and offer your gift.
>
> Matthew 5:23,24

After church, we got our boys, got in the van, and I was tempted to get mad again because I saw the coffee stains. But I didn't! Instead, I said, "Boys, I need you to forgive me. I shouldn't have treated your mom that way, and I shouldn't have lost my temper like that."

That day I taught them Matthew 5:23-24 without even quoting it, and they also learned a valuable lesson from Proverbs 24:16: the righteous man may fall seven times, but he gets right back up again. I was a living example to them of sinning, repenting, making it right with the ones you've offended, and going on with your life. And all of that happens when you utter those two powerful words, "Forgive me." This wasn't the first time I asked for their forgivness, and it certainly wouldn't be the last!

I gave my kids hope by asking them to forgive me. They could see that no matter how many times they trip, they can still get up, make it right, and keep going. They learned that those who really love God still miss it, but they also admit it and do what Jesus would do to get things straight: ask for forgiveness. When they do that, they don't stay down long. Soon, they're up on their feet, happy, and moving forward again.

If your kids hear you say, "Forgive me"—especially if the person you wronged was them—they will be more likely to not be stubborn and unrepentant when you confront them with their own sins and mistakes. If they see humility and truth operating in your life, you will find humility and truth operating in their lives.

## Be a Role Model

Josh McDowell recently reported that 41 percent of churchgoing kids today say that they have no role model to respect. Another 20 percent say that they might have a role model, but they're not sure. These percentages are higher than any other generation in the history of our nation—and that is frightening.[1] That means our kids are left without believers to look up to, Christians who exemplify what is good and decent and wise.

Teenagers are not looking for someone who says and does all the right things. They are looking for someone who puts their money where their mouth is, who actually practices what they preach. In fact, they would rather see it than hear about it. For a parent (or adult friend) to be a role model for a teenager, it takes courage. You have to be transparent and brutally honest with yourself and with them. Here are what I call the four B's of brave parents who really try to be a good, godly role model for their kids.

## Be Understanding

When kids do bonehead stuff and you're ready to throttle them, that's when you need to be cool and understanding. After you deal with what they did, tell them some of the silly things you did and the mistakes you made—and the price you paid for your stupidity. Explain how you felt and what you thought and how you learned some of the lessons the hard way.

It's even better if you can share these stories with them before they are in situations where they are tempted to do the same stupid thing you did. Tell them how you messed up, and also tell them the terrible consequences of your actions. Then tell them that you have high hopes for them, that they will be smarter than you were and learn from your mistakes. You will pray that they will remember the crazy thing their father or mother did, and when they face the same situation, they won't make that mistake themselves.

Kids love it when you are real with them. When you sit down and tell them about some of the traumas and problems you went through when you were their age, they can relate to you. It means a lot to kids when you say, "You know what? I understand what you're going through. Let me tell you what it was like when I was your age."

## Be Approachable

It takes real courage and self-restraint to stay in control when your kids say or do something that's out of line. I'm not saying that you shouldn't be strong, that you can never get angry or upset, or that you shouldn't enforce the rules. But you must stay open and available. Your teenagers should feel like they can talk to you and share things with you without fear that you will reject them or retaliate in a harmful way. They need to know that no matter what they've done or what kind of mess they are in—and no matter how upset you get—you will help them work through it and still love them. That's being an approachable parent.

If you've already lost it too many times, and your kids are afraid to talk to you, you can still regain their trust. First, you need to acknowledge your past over-reactions and ask them to forgive you. Second, you need to ask them to pray for you

> >

**With God's help, you can go from being an unapproachable parent to an approachable parent. It's never too late.**

because you are determined to change, but it is hard. Then, the next time they make a mistake or mouth-off or break the rules, you do what's right. Control your anger, confront them, discipline them, and pray with them. And if you haven't been letting them know about similar stuff you did as a kid, now's the time. With God's help, you can go from being an unapproachable parent to an approachable parent. It's never too late.

## Be Honest

Honesty is always the best policy with kids. When you blow it, tell them you blew it. When you don't have a clue, tell them when you're not sure about something and have to ask God and other people to help you figure it out. If they ask you a question and you don't know the answer, just say, "You know what? I don't know. Let me pray about that. Let me do some research." If you act like you always know the answer to everything, then when they don't know something, they won't know how to handle it. But if you openly admit you don't know something and then involve them in discovering the answer or the truth of the matter, especially when you're dealing with God's Word, it shows them that ignorance can be fixed and is nothing to be ashamed of. Being stupid is acting like you know something when you don't!

You also need to tell your kids that asking questions does not mean you're stupid. You need to explain the difference between being stupid and being ignorant.

The Bible says that we perish for a lack of knowledge, and that means believers should be gaining knowledge all the time. You can't gain knowledge without asking questions. You can't learn anything without admitting you don't know something first.

Humility in learning is a great character trait, and our kids need to see that at home; because in school, at work, and out in the world, people can laugh at them when they ask questions. When they don't know something other people think they ought to know, many of those people will make fun of them or tease them for their ignorance. There are even those who are so insecure that they make themselves feel better by embarrassing others because they ask questions or don't know something. Teach your kids early on that *that* is being stupid!

Our kids need to understand that being honest when we don't know something is smart. It is the way we go from being ignorant to being knowledgeable. If they see you do this at home, and they understand how the world operates, they won't have a problem asking questions and learning wherever they are. They won't let the devil cheat them out of what God has for them because they're too afraid to admit they don't know something and are afraid to ask someone about it.

## Be a Godly Example

Show your teenagers how to repent, how to recover, how to move forward, and how to live a life that is surrendered to Christ. Let them know what is going on in your life. Don't just ask them about theirs and never offer anything in return. They will be much more willing to confide in you if you confide in them from time to time. If you're having trouble getting along with someone at work, it's making you feel insecure, and as a result you are taking it out on your spouse and your kids, ask them to forgive you and then let them into your life. Tell them what's bugging you and ask them to pray for you.

Acting like you're perfect is not fooling anyone, especially your kids! Be understanding, be approachable, be honest, and be a godly example in your own life. Then your kids will be a lot more willing to let you into their lives and respect your authority over them.

# 6 Things Your Teens Must Believe About Themselves[2]

1.     I have been given power over the devil. (1 John 4:4.)

2.     I have been given power over every circumstance in my life. (Mark 11:23.)

3.     I have a strong body that has been healed by the stripes taken on Jesus' back. (Matt. 8:17.)

4.     I have the ability to control my mind and cast out evil thoughts. (2 Cor. 10:4,5.)

5.     I am poised for success and will not accept any defeat as final. (1 Cor. 15:57.)

6.     I hate sin but love all people and have favor everywhere I go. (Prov. 12:2.)

> >

Mother Nature is
providential. She gives us
twelve years to develop a
love for our children before
turning them
into teenagers.

William Calvin

Four

# "Lighten up!
# I'm not Billy Graham or
# Mother Teresa!"

I n the last chapter we dealt with the fact that parents are not perfect and shouldn't act like they are. But kids aren't perfect either, and parents have to deal with that head on. We all want our kids to be great. We burst with pride every time they do something spectacular and brag to our friends about them. Unfortunately, we also sink to the depths of despair or become furious when they embarrass us by saying or doing the wrong thing.

Teenagers often remind me that they are still learning and trying to figure out how to do life, and they need adults to understand that and give them some room to grow. As Christian parents we need to stop expecting our teenager to be another Billy Graham or Mother Teresa. They are unique individuals who are trying to discover who God made them to be and what He has called them to do. Furthermore, they are trying to figure out how to relate to us, to each other, and to the world at large. With all that going on, there are going to be times when their behavior will fall far short of any of the great men and women of faith we want them to be like.

What does "lighten up" really mean? What are our kids saying to us? They are simply asking us to have patience. And it's been my experience that in order to have patience, we also need to have endurance and perseverance. We must understand and accept what they are going through and determine to help them get past it and grow up—no matter what it takes or how long it takes.

Parenting a teenager is not a forty-yard dash. It is a cross-country marathon where only the strong survive. We have got to be in this thing for the long haul. I read the other day that raising teenagers is like raising cats. Neither teenagers nor cats turn their heads when you call them by name, and cats and teenagers can lie on the living room sofa for hours without moving, barely even breathing. Worse yet, it seems like it takes forever to get through to them.

You must have patience, endurance, and perseverance to get through to kids. It takes time for them to understand. It takes time and sometimes repeated effort on your part before you see them gradually take responsibility for their lives and achieve a healthy dependence on God and independence from you. You have to let out the rope wisely, slowly, and patiently, giving

them more and more freedom as they become more
and more responsible.

## Putting Away Childish Things

The apostle Paul put it this way.

> When I was a child, I spoke as a child, I understood
> as a child, I thought as a child: but when I became
> a man [or an adult], I put away childish things.
>
> 1 Corinthians 13:11

The Word of God reveals that there is a process of
moving from childhood to adulthood. Paul said that
in order to become a mature adult, he had to learn
how to put away his childish thinking, childish
talking, and childish behavior. The important thing
for us to remember is that it is a process and it takes
time. Therefore, it also takes patience, endurance,
and perseverance!

One of the biggest jobs of the parent is to patiently
work with their kids as they put away their childish
things, one thing at a time and sometimes several
things at a time. This is the process of moving from
adolescence to adulthood, and it is what a teenager's
life is all about. They want to grow up. They want to
get big. They want to do big things. They want to
have more money. They want to go out on their own.
They want to hang out with their friends. They are

struggling to establish their own life and identity apart from their family as well as within their family.

It is hard not to feel rejected when they do this, but you can't. You have to understand and be patient with them. That doesn't mean you don't take an active interest in what they are doing and who they are doing it with; it just means you give them as much room as you can to do that without your direct supervision.

When they were young, everywhere you went with your friends, there they were, toddling along with you. But now that they are older, they want to be with their friends. And their childish toys have become adult toys. They no longer race their toy cars across the floor. Now they want to get a real car and drive places with their friends and sometimes by themselves just to feel like they are their own person.

They want things and you want things to supervise their things. For example, they want a car and you want a global positioning satellite system to know where that car is at all times! They want money, so you tell them to get a job. They want a boyfriend or girlfriend who is cool. You want them to date the apostle Paul or the Virgin Mary. They want freedom and you want to see some sign that they are responsible. The struggle is finding the balance in all this, the balance of granting freedom and demanding responsibility as they move from childhood to adulthood.

One of the things that has helped me to gauge when my kids are ready for certain responsibilities and

>>

| Their Age | Who You Are to Them |
|---|---|
| 0-7 Child | Protector Commander Figurehead |
| 7-14 Adolescent | Provider Coach Fuddy-Duddy |
| 14-21 Young Adult | Propeller Counselor Friend |

> >

**Around fourteen your sweet kid disappears and in their place is standing a teenager who knows everything. They want to make all their decisions on their own, and they believe your role is to let them.**

activities is understanding the stages of growth they are going through. When you recognize these stages, it is much easier to either hold them back or let them go on because you know what their maturity level is, what they can and cannot handle.

## Three Stages of Growth

I believe there are three stages that our young people go through, and each of these stages is about seven years. The first is childhood. Childhood lasts from birth to about age seven. They are dependent upon you for nearly everything. You tell them when to get up, when to go to sleep, when they can play, when they should rest, what to wear, who they can play with, what to eat and when, and what to think about everything—God, family, church, work, play, country, people, and this world.

The next stage is adolescence, which begins around eight years old. Your kids go through a major change because they start to form their own opinions and their own personalities begin to emerge. They want to make more of their own decisions. They want to pick out their own clothes. Before they changed, you could put anything you wanted on them, tell them they looked great, and they were happy. After they change, they look in the mirror and say, "I don't like this dress. I want to wear jeans to church. Everybody else does."

In the beginning of the teenage years, during adolescence, a lot happens. The boys have more hair, their eyes and ears have gotten a little bigger, and they have this goofy smile on their face. The girls discover fashion and make-up and want to be like college girls and models in the magazines. And as they approach fourteen years of age, all are developing physically, mentally, emotionally, and sexually at a tremendous rate. They are trying to figure out how they fit into the scheme of things at home, at school, at church, and in the activities they are involved in. However, generally they are happy—and so are you. You're thinking how much you enjoy your kid.

Then something major happens. Around fourteen your sweet kid disappears and in their place is standing a teenager who knows everything. This is the young adulthood stage, which goes on from about fourteen to twenty-one. It is during this time that they want to put things on their body—aluminum, metal, heavy objects—and this is very challenging to you. They want to make all their decisions on their own, and they believe your role is to let them. In other words, you have become somewhat irrelevant unless they need something from you.

## Three Attitudes

As you go through these three stages, what you find is that your kids change the way they think about you. When they are ages one through seven—in the childhood stage—you're their protector. You watch over them. You care for them. You keep them out of traffic and away from junk food.

When they are seven to fourteen years old—during the adolescence stage—you're their provider. You drive them to all their lessons and sports events. You get them the basketball shoes or the trumpet they need to participate in the activities you take them to. And you make certain that they have adult supervision (yours or someone you trust) wherever they go in case they need something.

When they turn fourteen and even until they are finishing college at twenty-one—during the young adulthood stage—you're their propeller. You help them get where they want to go and help them to do what they want to do. You send them out into the world to be who God called them to be and do what He called them to do.

When they enter the adolescent stage, you may long for them to be children again, when you were their commander and there were no questions or mutinies. You just told them the way it was going to be and what they were going to do, and that's the way it went. If there was any kind of disobedience or rebellion, you disciplined them, instructed them, prayed with them, loved them through it—and all was well. It was common to hear them say, "Yes, Mommy. Yes, Daddy."

In adolescence, they begin to question your judgment a little bit more. You go from being commander to coach. They won't accept no without a reason. You have to tell them why they are to live a certain way or do things according to a particular standard. You have to work with them and train them. Then, if you've done your job as a commander and a coach, in their young adulthood they will look to you as their counselor.

As young adults, they have learned some things. They have observed how different people live and the consequences of their choices. They will want you to give them advice when they are making big decisions. They may not take your advice, but they still want it.

In these three stages your kids will also change the way they see you. When they are children, they look to you as a figurehead. You are the governor of their home, their leader, their fearless commander who knows everything just because you are so old.

When they become adolescents, you go from being the figurehead to the fuddy-duddy. You're not too sharp anymore. You don't quite know it all. They figure out that you are still figuring some things out. But if you really work with them and take the time to develop a good relationship with them, by the time they get to the young adult stage, you will have become one of their most trusted friends. You have a

> >

If we've done our job as our kids
are growing up, if we've been
there to guide them, to lead
them, to coach them, to train
them, to spend time with them,
and to encourage them in all
God has called them to be and
do; then their young adult years,
especially the latter part, can be
terrific years.

friendship that is based on years of honesty, under-standing, patience, respect—and in all this have shown your love for them.

## We Are Not the World

Today, television and movies portray teenagers, espe-cially older teenagers, as disrespecting, distrusting, and even hating their parents. This is the opposite of the biblical view of the way it ought to be—and the way it can be. If we've done our job as our kids are growing up, if we've been there to guide them, to lead them, to coach them, to train them, to spend time with them, and to encourage them in all God has called them to be and do; then their young adult years, especially the latter part, can be terrific years. They still respect you as a parent, but your relationship has grown into a friendship, a camaraderie of love and trust.

What does it take to get to the place where they are twenty-one and you are one of their closest friends, confidants, and counselors? Patience, endurance, and perseverance! And those character attributes are vital because we are raising our kids in a world that is opposed to the truth of the gospel of Jesus Christ. It's just that simple. To raise teenagers who love God and serve Him with all their heart, soul, mind, and strength in today's world is no small task.

Our kids have to be taught that the standards of a child of God are different than the standards of the world in which they interact every day. They must understand that following Jesus Christ and living according to His Word and the Holy Spirit may not win them popularity contests. Most kids love the challenge of standing for truth against tremendous opposition, however. And if they see you fight the good fight of faith and their personal relationship with Jesus is strong, they will gladly reject the deceptions and lies of the world to live for the Lord.

On the other hand, if you don't teach them how to overcome the world, the devil, and their own carnality through the grace and strength of God's Word and His Spirit, and if you don't fight the good fight of faith yourself, then chances are your kids will not either. They will gravitate toward worldly thinking and standards and eventually fall away from God altogether. So in the process of giving them more and more responsibility and freedom as they grow older, always teach them God's Word and encourage them to live by His Spirit.

## The Process of Leaving

The word "adolescent" is a combination of two Latin words, which mean to grow up and to be nourished.[1] We are to see that our kids increase in knowledge and wisdom by feeding them all the good things in life.

The most important thing we feed our kids, of course, is God's Word. Giving them God's Word as we go about our daily lives is what connects them to God. And all this is preparing us and them for the day when they will leave us and start a family of their own. This is why kids are always seeking more freedom, more "space."

In Mark 10:7 Jesus says, "For this reason a man shall leave his father and mother and be joined to his wife." What this tells parents is that we are training our teenagers to be able to leave us and be able to form a family of their own. Adolescence is a process of leaving to establish another family for God.

Although we want them to be able to leave us physically and have a healthy and godly independence, we never want them to leave us spiritually. We always want them to share our faith in Jesus Christ. With this in mind, I have learned a major truth for parenting teenagers: If we don't allow them to leave gradually through the patient process of growing freedoms matched by heightened accountability, when they do finally leave, it's unlikely they'll ever come back. In other words, if we hold on and don't allow them to gradually gain more freedom and earn more of our trust, they will leave like a bird escaping from a cage and never want to return.

The American Family in Crisis and Southern Baptist Council on Family Life did a study that revealed some disturbing facts. They found out that 88 percent of the children raised in evangelical homes leave the church at eighteen years of age and never return! Somehow these parents are missing it. They're failing to do what is necessary to connect with their kids and see that their kids are properly connected to Jesus and His body.

In Proverbs 22:6 the Bible tells us that if we train or coach our children in the way they should go—having faith and trust in Jesus Christ—then when they are older they won't depart. They won't leave Jesus or His church. That doesn't mean they'll never make a mistake, have times of testing, change denominations, or question some of their beliefs. But they will never make a conscious decision to say, "I reject the faith of my parents. Jesus is no longer my Lord and I no longer want to fellowship with other believers."

## Five Ways To Earn Freedom

How can we help our young people earn more freedom? How can we help them to leave gracefully through their older teenage years? Here are five things that I tell my kids, which seem to have a great impact on them.

### 1.     Take your freedom in steps, not leaps.

So you want to increase your curfew. If you are faith-ful to be in at ten on Friday nights for six months, then we will make it eleven for the next six months. Let's set reachable goals that can lead to greater freedom and more adult responsibility. I'm not going to rush you, and you must get used to one level of responsi-bility before you go to the next.

## 2. Never take your freedoms for granted or you'll lose them.

Respect and appreciate the freedoms I have given you and the new opportunities you've earned as you show you can handle them. Life is not a game, and what you are doing is not trivial. Accepting the responsibility for each new freedom is so important because each time you do represents another stepping stone to reaching maturity and integrity.

## 3. As a parent I have the right to find out if you are abusing the freedom I've given you.

I have the right to check up on you. It is my duty to find out if you were where you said you were. I can put a GPS system on your car if I want to. I can call and make sure that you are really at a friend's house and the parents are at home. I have a right to smell your breath after you've been to a party and to go through your drawers and closet to make certain you have not fallen into drinking or drugs. Because you are still young and under my care, I have the right and the responsibility to make you accountable to me.

> >

**Your kids are saying, "Lighten up!" because they want you to enjoy them as you train them to leave you.**

## 4.     You've got to think before you act.

If you want more freedoms, you've got to think, to process risk and look at the possible consequences of your actions. Teenagers usually just think about what they're going to do, what they want to do, and what they're friends are doing, without thinking about the long-term. I want you to move from instant gratification thinking to action and reaction thinking. Think: *If I say or do this, what will happen? What are the possibilities—good, bad, and ugly? Most important, is this something God wants me to do?*

## 5.     If you want more freedom, you must prove that you can govern and discipline yourself.

You've got to show me that you are making decisions to govern your life, that you are controlling your emotions and disciplining your mind and body. I shouldn't have to tell you to do your homework. Your mother shouldn't have to tell you to clean up after yourself. Once curfews are set, we shouldn't have to remind you of them, nor should we have to get you up in the morning. When we see you govern and discipline yourself in your daily life, we will gladly give you more freedom.

## Enjoy the Process

Your kids are also saying, "Lighten up!" because they want you to enjoy them as you train them to leave you. This is a hard order to fill because we want them to be with us forever—most of the time (sometimes we want them to be out of the house yesterday)! And, while they appreciate the high expectations that you have of them, they want room to grow and reasonable growth at a reasonable pace.

If we understand the three major stages of growth; let them have freedoms as they prove themselves responsible and mature enough; and work on patience, endurance, and perseverance—with them and with ourselves—there is a great possibility that we can actually enjoy the process!

One thing is certain, however; it is impossible for us to trust our kids with their own lives. We can only do what God leads us to do and trust Him. We must go to the foundations of our faith in Him: He knows what's best for each time and situation of their lives, and He will never let us down. In reality, obeying and trusting God is the only way we can enjoy the process of letting go and then watch them go out on their own. Without His love, grace, and exceeding great and precious promises, I doubt any of us could handle our kids growing older and becoming independent from us. But with His help, we can do all things—even let them go!

# 3 Stereotypes Your Teen Must Overcome as a Follower of Jesus Christ[2]

1. "Christians think they're all perfect." We overcome this stereotype by being quick to acknowledge God's grace and forgiveness in our lives. Paul reminded the church that he was chief of all sinners! We must humbly acknowledge that without God's incredible mercy, we would be lost and that we need His help every moment of every day.

2. "Christians think they know everything." We conquer this stereotype by simply being honest when we don't have an answer for someone. If your teen is talking about God with a friend and they bring up something they're not sure about, they can just admit they don't know the answer but will do some research and try to find out. Not knowing everything

about God doesn't make Him any less real to His children. After all, we do know Him.

3. "Christians don't have any fun." This one is easy. Tell your young person to have fun and enjoy life. Fun isn't getting drunk or high, nor is it getting into bed with a new person every weekend. Fun is having great friends who don't need artificial activities to enjoy life. There is no greater "high" than knowing and being in the presence of Almighty God!

>>

Children seldom misquote you. In fact, they usually repeat word for word what you shouldn't have said.

Anonymous

Five

# "'Because I said so,' isn't good enough."

Always be ready to give a logical defense to anyone who asks you to account for the hope that is in you, but do it courteously and respectfully

1 Peter 3:15 AMP

The Bible tells us to give a good and reasonable explanation for what we believe, and that includes our kids. We have to help them understand why we believe what we believe, why we live the way we do, and why we require certain things of them. Asking for blind obedience of a child—when they are three or four years old—is going to work. But if you expect blind obedience when they are thirteen or fourteen—without explaining why—it will produce rebellion. We must always give some explanation for the rules and guidelines that we set for them.

## Communication Is Everything

We must learn to communicate our life values in a way that our kids can understand. It's important to relate our beliefs to them by putting ourselves in their shoes. I'm going to tell you a story that illustrates this principle. A three-year-old boy was eating an apple in the backseat of a car, and his father was driving. He said, "Daddy, why is my apple turning brown?"

> >

**Teenagers need to know the "why," not just the "what," and we have a responsibility to see that they understand why we are requiring certain things of them.**

His dad looked at his little son and said, "Well, after you ate the skin off, the meat of the apple came into contact with the air, which caused it to oxidize; thus changing the molecular structure and turning it a different color."

There was a long silence, and the son asked softly, "Daddy, are you talking to me?"

That's the way our teenagers feel when we don't take the time to explain things on their level. Sometimes it takes thought and effort on our part to figure out how to explain what we mean. The Bible warns us that this is vitally important with kids. When they cannot understand what we are

74

communicating to them, either they will think we are making them feel stupid or they will be frustrated and angry. Either way, if we communicate poorly or have a lack of consideration for their age and level of understanding, we will only make the problem worse.

> And you, fathers, do not provoke your children to wrath, but bring them up in the training and admonition of the Lord.
>
> Ephesians 6:4

What this is telling us is that we must not only say the right thing, but we must say it in the right way. If you tell your teenagers they can't do something and give no explanation, then you will provoke them and make them angry and upset. Teenagers need to know the "why," not just the "what," and we have a responsibility to see that they understand why we are requiring certain things of them.

Jesus said, "When anyone hears the word of the kingdom, and does not understand it, then the wicked one comes and snatches away what was sown in his heart" (Matt. 13:19). So we've got a responsibility to make sure that when we teach our kids the Word, they understand it, that they're getting it. Josh MacDowell said it best.

Number 1: We teach the precept.

Number 2: We teach the principle.

> >

**What they believe determines how they live their lives. What they believe also determines their values and their values determine their actions.**

Number 3: We teach the person.

As we help our teenagers grow up, a lot of times we stop at the precept. The precept is what they need to do. But we need to go to the next step and explain why they are to do something. That is the principle. For example, I will say to my kids, "It says in 1 Corinthians 6:18 that we are to flee immorality. I want you to live a pure life. I want you to keep your body pure. I don't want you getting into trouble sexually." I just gave them the precept. I told them what I wanted them to do. Now, what is the principle behind the precept, or why should they flee sexual immorality?

The principle behind this precept is that God created sex in the context of love and marriage. Sex is most pleasurable, remains pure, and has no bad consequences when it remains within the covenant of marriage. If you have sex outside of marriage, you open yourself up for all kinds of trouble, including disease and emotional problems. God gave us Scriptures like 1 Corinthians 6:18 for our own protection and pleasure.

I have given them the precept and the principle. Now that brings me to the person, and the person is God. I tell them, "God loves you. He's pure and He's faithful to you. If He asks you to be faithful to your wife or to your husband, then He will be faithful to bring you the right mate at the right time. He's going to be faithful to reward your faithfulness and purity."

When you communicate clearly and do your best not to provoke your teenagers to wrath, you build trust with them. And when your teenagers trust you, they know that you will always tell them the truth—and the whole truth.

## The Truth Makes You Free

It's really ironic that kids will put you through the wringer when you tell them they can't do something. They need to know why, and the reason better be a good one. But when it comes to knowing spiritual truth, knowing what you believe and why you believe it, they think that's for preachers and parents. One of the things I tell the kids at Oneighty as well as my own kids is that you have to know what you believe. You have to have an understanding of truth. Why? Because the foundation of their lives is their beliefs.

Human beings will never make a decision that is outside of what they believe to be true. What they believe determines how they live their lives. What they believe also determines their values—which is what they believe is right and what they believe is wrong—

and their values determine their actions. Actions speak louder than words when it comes to what you believe.

Let's say you believe the Bible is the Word of God, and the Bible says, "Thou shalt not lie." That's one of the Ten Commandments. If you really believe it is God's Word, then not lying will be a core value in your life and your behavior will be honest. You believe God's Word, which says that lying is bad; and as a result you value honesty. The result of valuing honesty is that you are an honest person. You respect honesty in others. And you will not lie, even when it hurts you. You are committed to the truth.

Why is this so important? How does this affect your life? You will never be fired from a job because you lied. You will never be expelled from school because you cheated on a test. Your spouse, kids, friends, and family will trust you because you are always honest with them. You are going to save yourself from all kinds of pain and problems not only because you know what you believe, but also because you believe the right things—God's Word—and your values and actions reflect what you believe.

If you decide you don't believe God's Word, you believe instead that it is okay to lie, you give no value to honesty, and you lie habitually, you will suffer for it. You may lose a job or be cut from a sports team because you lied. You may not pass a class because you cheated, and if this goes on your high school record, you may not get into the college of your choice. Your spouse, kids, friends, and family will not trust you because you have lied to them. The result of your decision to not believe God's Word, which says that lying is a sin and therefore wrong behavior, is a lot of pain and suffering in your life.

What we need to get through to kids is that God didn't write the Bible to make our lives miserable. He wrote it so that we could have the wisdom and strength to do right and accomplish His will for our lives—which is the only way we can be happy and fulfilled in life. He made us and He knows what will give us pleasure and satisfaction.

## Demonstrate and Illustrate

When you are teaching kids, you have to illustrate your point. Demonstrating what you're trying to get across to them not only shows them how life works in a tangible way, but also it emphasizes the importance of what you are saying to them.

One day I illustrated the value and importance of sexual purity in our youth group by using a couple of cans of Coke. First, I took a warm can of Coke, popped it open, and asked one of the kids if he'd like to have a drink of it. He said yes and took a drink. Then I asked another teenager, "Would you like a drink?" She said yes and took a drink. I continued to pass the can around until there was only a little left, and about four kids had taken a drink from it. At that point there was nothing but backwash left.

I said, "Who'd like to finish it off?" Very few kids wanted to, but there was one bold, big guy who yelled, "I'll do it!" He slugged it down. Kids were screaming, getting grossed out, and the kid who was drinking the dregs of the Coke was doing it to be seen and to make a scene. When he was finished I took the empty can and put it down in front of me, where they all could see it. Then I reached into a cooler full of ice and pulled out a fresh can of ice-cold Coke. I held it up and I said, "You know what? I'm not going to share this with anyone. I'm not going to pass this around. And I'd like to know something. Is there one teenager here who would like to polish off this can of Coke all by yourself?"

> >

**Show them what the Bible says and challenge them to study it and seek God for themselves if they don't agree with you or have some problem with it.**

Every kid in the place started hollering, "I will! I will!" They all wanted that can of Coke. Finally, I invited one kid to come up, and he drank it all down. The kids cheered him on as he was drinking, and he finished with a big smile on his face. What kids get excited about always amazes me.

I said, "Listen, guys. When you get married one day, God wants you to be a fresh can of Coke. He doesn't want you to be an emotional, sexual, spiritual

80

backwash because you messed around with every person who came into your life romantically. If you do that, by the time you do meet the right one, you will have so much impurity in your life you won't know what to think or do. You might not even recognize the right one for you. That's why God wants you to be clean. He wants you to be pure. He wants you to be that fresh can of Coke on your marriage night. If you've already messed up, God will forgive your sin and give you a brand-new start. No matter where you are in this, let's make a commitment of purity to Him right now and keep it."

The reaction of the kids to my simple demonstration was awesome. For the first time some of them finally figured it out. "Oh. I get it! That's why it says, 'flee fornication.' That's why it says, 'when you commit sexual immorality, you're hurting your own body'! You're getting backwash into your body. We don't want that. We want to be pure. I want to be a fresh can of Coke!"

Of course, one big kid came up to me after the meeting and said, "Pastor Blaine, can I be a fresh can of *Diet* Coke?" But he got the point!

## Getting Them To Think

To sum up, here are five things to help you get your point across when dealing with the adolescent brain.

## 1.     Let them explain their position.

"Tell me what you think. How are you seeing this issue? I want to hear what's in your heart concerning this problem. You just go ahead and let it all out." Then you listen carefully. You'll be able to identify exactly where they are and what they're thinking, what they've been going through, and what their friends have been telling them. And, most important, you'll know what to say and do. If they are okay, you can compliment them and reward them. If they are out to lunch, you can develop a strategy with the Holy Spirit to bring them around.

## 2.     Tell them the "why" and the "who" and not just "what."

Help them to understand the reason for what you are asking or commanding them to do, always bringing in God's point of view. Show them what the Bible says and challenge them to study it and seek God for themselves if they don't agree with you or have some problem with it.

## 3.     Let them ask questions.

After you've talked about it and given them the "why" and the "who," don't stop there. Let them raise questions or ask them if they have any questions. Then work with them. If you don't know the answer, say so, and do the research together.

## 4.    Learn to illustrate and demonstrate.

Jesus was a great illustrator. If you read the Sermon on the Mount out loud, as if Jesus were actually teaching it, you would find out that it lasted sixteen minutes from start to finish. In the process of the sixteen minutes, He used sixty-seven different illustrations, which is about 4.2 illustrations per minute. He was a master illustrator. He wanted people to see a natural example of a spiritual truth—and He still does!

## 5.    Work through the process until you come into agreement.

You've found out what their position is. You've explained the "what," the "why," and the "who." You've let them ask questions. You've illustrated and demonstrated every way you can think. Then you continue to work through that process until you come into agreement. This is critical. You and your teenager have to understand the truth and agree to the truth if it takes five minutes or five hours. You can't let them go on their way and still be at odds with you and the Word of God.

After you have come into agreement, you can pray together to seal the deal with the Holy Spirit. When you take the time to go through this process with your kids, they know that if they go out and do the right thing, they will be one step closer to getting more freedom. But more important, they will have the peace of mind that can only come from knowing what they believe and why they believe it—and you will be able to send them forth with trust and confidence.

# 7 Scriptures To Guide Your Teen's Future[1]

1.  Jeremiah 29:11: "For I know the thoughts that I think toward you, says the Lord, thoughts of peace and not of evil, to give you a future and a hope."

2.  Jeremiah 33:3: "Call to Me, and I will answer you, and show you great and mighty things, which you do not know."

3.  Joshua 1:8: "This Book of the Law shall not depart from your mouth, but you shall meditate in it day and night, that you may observe to do according to all that is written in it. For then you will make your way prosperous, and then you will have good success."

4.  Proverbs 18:16: "A man's gift makes room for him, and brings him before great men."

5. Ephesians 3:20: "Now to Him who is able to do exceedingly abundantly above all that we ask or think, according to the power that works in us."

6. 2 Timothy 1:9: "Who has saved us and called us with a holy calling, not according to our works, but according to His own purpose and grace which was given to us in Christ Jesus before time began."

7. Ephesians 5:15: "See then that you walk circumspectly, not as fools but as wise."

> >

If kids clearly see the promises, they will gladly pay the price.

Anonymous

Six

# "Give me direction because I've never been where I'm going."

Today's teenager is going into a world that they've never experienced. They're attempting things and doing things that they've never done. Maybe you remember what it was like when you were growing up and you didn't know what it was like to have a girlfriend or boyfriend. You didn't know what it was like to have a job, a paycheck, a bank account—and a hundred dollars in your bank account. And what about driving a car for the first time?

Everything is new for a young person. They continually experience new things, and they want to know how to do these things right. They want to be successful. They want to make the right decisions. Unfortunately, they often make their choices according to where they are getting their information. Some get input from their parents and take their parents seriously, but every teenager really wants their parents to give them the knowledge and wisdom they need to be successful in life.

Most kids get their information from their classes in school, television, the Internet, magazines, and their peers. There is nothing wrong with becoming knowledgeable about the world in this way. Facts, in and of themselves, will not harm them and may actually give them answers to some of their questions. But knowledge without the foundation of truth from the Bible and the divine leading of the Holy Spirit can get a kid into tremendous trouble. Unless they have the wisdom of God to put all that information in proper perspective, they are lost. And that wisdom comes as they study the Bible, follow the Holy Spirit, listen to their godly parents, and glean from other Christian friends and elders.

> >

**Kids today want to be spiritual. They want to know God. They have a deep yearning and hunger to do the right things and to be spiritual people, but they don't have the right information.**

Whether our kids seem to want our input or not, God specifically calls us to train our kids to rely on His Word and His Spirit. We are the ones He

90

expects to get them the right information and point them in the right direction.

## How Are We Doing?

Here are a few statistics from the Barna Research Group that you might find interesting.

1.  Among teenagers, what we see is that we will continue to get from them well-intentioned but misinformed faith perspectives that lead to bad choices and spiritual confusion.

2.  Eighty-six percent of teenagers who claim to be Christian are confused about their Christian beliefs and are theologically complacent.

3.  Sixty percent of these young people, who claim to be followers of Christ, believe that their salvation is earned by work.

4.  Two-thirds of the teenagers in America believe that Satan is a symbol of evil rather than a living, real being.

5.  Fifty-three percent of Christian young people surveyed believe that Jesus was not actually perfect.[1]

This tells us that kids today want to be spiritual. They want to know God. They have a deep yearning and hunger to do the right things and to be spiritual people, but they don't have the right information. They believe that they are Christians but are confused about what a Christian believes and how a Christian should live.

From this survey, the majority of teenagers believe that in order to get into heaven, they have to prove themselves to God. This is what the Bible calls dead works. Yes, James 2:14-26 tells us that faith without works is dead, but James is talking about *after* we are saved. We are first saved by faith, and then our works must be inspired by faith in God and led by His Spirit and His Word. Works alone will not save anyone. Why? Because then redemption and reconciliation to God are based on our works instead of the redemptive work of Jesus. (See Ephesians 2:8-9.)

> >

**When young people have no vision to see down the road, they don't know how to live their lives. Their present has meaning only when they see the purpose and plan of their future.**

If teenagers are not being taught the basic foundations of the faith such as being saved by grace through faith in the shed blood of Jesus, then it is no mystery why they are so confused. Furthermore, if a kid doesn't believe Satan is a being to contend with, they will not recognize the enemy's attacks or know how to overcome them. This makes them vulnerable to demonic activity and oppression. And where did kids in this survey get the idea that there had to be a time during Jesus' life on earth when He sinned? If they got it from a movie or a book of fiction, their parents and church youth leaders didn't do anything to correct their ignorance.

Do you see that we have a generation of young people who are really hungry for spirituality, to find out what spiritual life is all about, but they're getting very little biblical truth? That means parents and churches are not doing what God directed them to do: train up their children in the way they should go.

When the Word of God is not taught at home, not only do kids have no firm foundation for faith in God, but they also have no direction in their lives. That's why we have a whole generation of young people who, through all their rebellion, disrespect, and acting out, are crying, "Give me direction!" Without God in their lives, they have no solid direction, no peace that passes all understanding that they are on the right path and doing the right thing.

## Kids Need a Vision

> Where there is no vision, the people perish: but he
> that keepeth the law, happy is he.
>
> Proverbs 29:18 KJV

Young people need a vision, but of all the young people on this planet, those in the Church should have the greatest vision and sense of purpose. The Bible says that without vision, the people perish. They have no ability to see down the road. And when young people have no vision to see down the road, they don't know how to live their lives. Their present has meaning only when they see the purpose and plan of their future.

When teenagers have a vision for their future they will make decisions that are going to be for their good. Why? Because they want to do the right thing, make a difference, and impact their world. They want to take the steps necessary to win their race. Show a kid the prize, and they will run to win. When our teenagers know and understand the promises of God, they will live their lives for God knowing that their love for Him and faithfulness to Him will bring great rewards in this life and for eternity.

Kids must be taught that blessings flow into their lives because they obey the Word of God and follow the Holy Spirit, have pure hearts before Jesus Christ, treat their friends right, and respect authority. God protects them, provides for them, gives them joy, peace, and fulfillment—and life is an adventure. If they see these promises, then they will passionately and happily pay the price to live a life that honors God.

Parents are not only responsible to teach their kids the Word of God, but along with that is the responsibility to impart God's vision for their lives into them. The world's philosophy of parenting today is, "Let your kids figure it out on their own. Educate them, then let them choose their own beliefs." There is a truth in that. Ultimately they will choose what they believe and how they will live. They have free will. But the Word of God gives a completely opposite view to parenting. God's Word says that we have a responsibility to provide spiritual direction.

Proverbs 22:6 says that parents are to train up their children in the way they should go. Notice, it does not say "in the way they want to go," "in the way their friends go," or "in the way the world says to go." It clearly states that there is a way they should go—ONE way. If we had any doubts, Jesus cleared it all up when He said in John 14:6, "I am THE way."

Proverbs 22:6 goes on to say that if we train them up in the way they should go—the way of Jesus Christ—then when they are old they will not depart from it. God is saying, "You know what? I want you to help your kids. I don't want you to leave them alone or throw them to the wolves in the world. I want you to guide your young people. Guide them to Me."

> And the LORD said, "Shall I hide from Abraham what I am doing, since Abraham shall surely become a great and mighty nation, and all the nations of the earth shall be blessed in him? For I have known him, in order that he may command his children and his household after him, that they keep the way of the LORD, to do righteousness and justice, that

the LORD may bring to Abraham what He has spoken to him."

Genesis 18:17-19

God says, "I'm going to tell Abraham what I'm doing," not because Abraham is such a great guy or even because he's got faith in Him. No, God trusts Abraham because he will "command his children and his household after him, that they will keep the way of the Lord."

The reason that God chose Abraham to be a father of our faith is because He knew that this man would give spiritual direction to every person in his household. He knew that this man would instruct his kids in the ways of the Lord. He knew that when Isaac—the promised son—came, Abraham would give him a godly spiritual education, teaching him to live according to God's Word—and a powerful vision for his life.

## Blessings for You Too

This is amazing! God chose Abraham because he could trust him to teach his children and grandchildren the Word of God. And then He made Abraham a father of many nations, both spiritual and natural. Abraham was perhaps more influential in the world's history than anyone except Jesus Himself.

Think about it. Abraham was the first Jew and the nation of Israel came from his line. Abraham also was the father of Ishmael and the Arab nations. Most important, his line brought forth the Messiah, Jesus, on whom we believe for salvation. But it all started with a man who would teach his children God's Word and require them to walk in it.

Do you know that when you make a solemn commitment to give spiritual direction to your kids, God marks you? He says, "I'm going to make you a leader. I'm going to bless you. I will give you favor and influence, which will open doors of opportunity for you. If I can trust you with My kids, then I can trust you with other things."

Not only does God bless you in your outward life, but He blesses you in your relationship with Him. In Genesis 18:19, God says, "For I have known him," and He's referring to Abraham. The Hebrew word translated "known" is the word *yada,* and it means "to ascertain by seeing." It also can mean observation, care, and recognition.[2] It implies a close friendship. God was saying that He had a special relationship with Abraham. He knew him inside

> >

**The blessings God has for you go on in your lifetime and for many generations to come, but when you train up your children and your children's children in the way they should go, it also affects your community and your nation.**

and out, and He knew that Abraham would raise his kids the way He wanted him to raise them.

## Train Up a Kid and Change Your Nation

The blessings God has for you go on in your lifetime and for many generations to come, but when you train up your children and your children's children in the way they should go, it also affects your community and your nation. God wanted Abraham to keep Isaac in the right path because other folks were not doing that, particularly in two cities called Sodom and Gomorrah. They were in such a sinful state that God could not allow them to continue or else they would contaminate other cities.

Sodom actually means "to scorch; burnt,"[3] and Gomorrah actually means "a ruined heap; chastised with piling blows."[4] Even the world is well aware of God's destruction of these infamous cities because they were so evil. And God did not want Abraham's household and especially Isaac to end up in Sodom and in Gomorrah.

Today America bears a great resemblance to Sodom and Gomorrah in many ways. Sin and evil abound here, primarily because generations of Christians did not train their kids in the way they should go. And God doesn't want our kids in a spiritual Sodom and Gomorrah. He doesn't want them scorched and burned in eternal hellfire. He doesn't want them walking in a sinful lifestyle, where He has to chastise with piling blows, and they must go through all kinds of difficulty.

I'm sure you know many people who are messed up adults. They are addicted to drugs or alcohol. They're hooked on pornography. They can't be faithful to one person in marriage, so after a series of divorces they just go from partner to partner. They're lying, cheating, and even committing crimes to get rich quick. How do these people end up this way? What is the root cause?

A large part of these problems goes back to how they were raised by their parents. Their parents either didn't know Jesus and have His wisdom to raise them, or they knew Him but didn't obey His Word regarding their kids. They may not have loved their kids enough or had the courage to give them instruction in right-eousness and require them to know and live by God's Word.

One fact must be faced. It takes courage to live your life and raise your kids according to the Word of God in America today. The Church is growing and gaining more ground in educa-tion, government, and other

> >

**God wants His young people to be a testimony in their world. He wants the world to look at His kids and say, "How did these kids turn out so well?"**

99

areas. However, the devil is not lying down and rolling over. He isn't just going to give up. He's made a lot of progress in the last fifty years, and he will not give up the territory he's won without a fight.

It takes pure guts to raise godly children in today's modern society, but the rewards are well worth the persecution and the difficulties. And training our kids in the ways of God is at the heart of what Jesus told us we were to do: make disciples of all nations.

What will happen to your kids if you take a loving, strong hand and give them direction, instruct them in the ways of the Lord, exhort them to follow the Holy Spirit, and teach them God's Word? What's the pay-off? Since Abraham is our prototype, let's see how Isaac did.

> Then Isaac sowed in that land, and reaped in the same year a hundredfold; and the LORD blessed him. The man began to prosper, and continued prospering until he became very prosperous; for he had possessions of flocks and possessions of herds and a great number of servants. So the Philistines envied him.
>
> Genesis 26:12-14

Years after growing up under Abraham, we find Isaac sowing, reaping, prospering, being blessed of God, and so wealthy that the entire Philistine nation envied him. How would you like your teenager to be the envy of their world in whatever career they chose?

God wants His young people to be a testimony in their world. He wants the world to look at His kids and say, "How did these kids turn out so well?" And when they ask, your kids will give honor and glory to God because of the principles that they learned from their parents as they were growing up.

What happened to Isaac can happen to your teenagers. You just need to do what Abraham did and train them in the ways of the Lord.

## Just How Much Direction Do You Give?

How do you do this? I want to give you a principle called One Minute Parenting, and I got it right from the Bible. Here's the same passage from Deuteronomy 6 that we looked at earlier from *The Message* translation.

> Write these commandments that I've given you today on your hearts. Get them inside of you and then get them inside your children. Talk about them wherever you are, sitting at home or walking in the street; talk about them from the time you get up in the morning to when you fall into bed at night. Tie them on your hands and foreheads as a reminder; inscribe them on the doorposts of your homes and on your city gates.
>
> Deuteronomy 6:6-9 MESSAGE

Notice that before we can do anything with our kids, we need to get the Word of God in ourselves. If we read, study, and meditate on God's Word, there is an excellent chance our children will do the same. If we don't do these things, there is an excellent chance they won't either.

God tells us that we are to teach our children the Word and talk about the Word continuously throughout their daily activities. We are literally to write the Word on ourselves and our houses. In other words, we are to live God's Word before them. The Word of God is to be everywhere, at all times, guiding us in all situations. He gives us eight ways to get His Word into the lives of young people.

## 1.　　Sitting at home.

Even if you are watching television together, ask them questions or make comments that will cause them to compare what they are watching with what God's Word has to say. You don't need to have a three-hour discussion. Just take a minute to relate what you are experiencing to biblical principles.

## 2.　　Walking in the street.

Some families take walks together, and that's a good time to have discussions about various topics that interest your teenager and slip in a one-minute message here and there. But when are you usually in the street? When you're driving. Pray and speak the Word of God over them as you drive them to school,

> >

A military ritual of family devotions
was never God's main plan. His idea
of imparting the Word was to give it
in bite-size pieces during the day
and let your kids chew on it for a
while. Then your kids will remember
special moments you had with them
instead of a long, tedious devotional
time that they dreaded every day!

a sports event, or a music lesson. Relate the Word to anything they are concerned about.

## 3.     When you get up in the morning.

When you're having breakfast, say a quick prayer to bless the meal and have a great day. Talk about what you are facing that day and remind your teenager how blessed they are.

## 4.     When you go to bed at night.

Kids always sleep much better when you pray over them or with them at bedtime. Ephesians 4:26 says that we should not go to sleep filled with anger, so this is the time to make certain your teenagers have forgiven all those who have offended and hurt them.

## 5.     Tie them on your hands.

What do we put on our hands? Rings and bracelets. In our church we give our young people a purity ring when they graduate from the discipleship program. It's something they can put on their hands to remind them of their commitment to be sexually pure. Teenagers are always putting some kind of bracelet on. The "WWJD"—what would Jesus do—bracelets were very popular for a while.

## 6.     Tie them on their foreheads.

Today we wear ball caps. We've got Oneighty ball caps, and there are all kinds of Christian ball caps that have things on them to remind kids of who they are in Christ, what they believe, and the great calling on their lives.

## 7.  Inscribe them on the doorposts of your homes.

Many Christians have welcome mats or plaques that have Scriptures written on them. But doorposts can also be the frame of your computer, the refrigerator door, the bathroom walls, and other places where you can put Scripture verses.

## 8.  Inscribe them on the city gates.

The Bible says that even when you go into the world, into the city, you can help them to remember God. First, by taking them to church, you are taking them out in the world to a place where God's Word is taught, believed, honored, and lived. And when you get to know the history of your city, you can teach your kids what the godly and ungodly influences have been through the years and how that has brought the city to where it is today.

Most of these things take just a minute to do. Many parents may do a long devotional every night. That can wear their kids out and bore them. They get tired of it and begin to resent the things of God. A military ritual of family devotions was never God's main plan. We can see from this passage in Deuteronomy 6 that His idea of imparting the Word was to give it in bite-size pieces during the day and let your kids chew on it for a while. Then your kids will remember special moments you had with them instead of a long, tedious devotional time that they dreaded every day!

## What About Discipline?

We know kids are looking for direction from their parents in spiritual matters, but what about good old-fashioned discipline? There was a study of American students from the seventh grade through the twelfth grade several years ago. The researchers found out the top things that kids think are the major problems in society today. Number 4 on their list was a lack of parental discipline!

You would think that high school kids would never have even thought of parental discipline. Wouldn't you expect them to say, "Oh, man! We love not having discipline. We like it when our parents ignore us and let us do what we want to do." But they didn't say that. They said, "We want parental direction and discipline."

How do we give our young people correction or discipline? If there's an adjustment that needs to be made with our teenager, how do we do that? How do we do it in the right way? We find some of the answers in another survey, in which one hundred thousand teenagers across the nation were asked what they wanted most from their parents. Here are some of their responses:

>>

Young people may act like they
wish you lived on a different planet,
but they really want your guidance
and direction when it comes to their
spiritual lives. They also want your
correction and discipline when it
comes to their natural lives.

1.   Answer our questions.

2.   Don't fight with us.

3.   Never lie to us.

4.   Praise our good points.

What they are basically asking for is real personal interaction with their parents. They want good, honest communication. They're crying out for their parents to talk to them, but they also want them to speak the truth in love. Following are seven mistakes that parents make in correcting or disciplining their kids.

## 1.   **They talk down to their kids.**

This can be with an attitude or through body language. If you are taller than your kid or standing when they are sitting or lying down, you will seem to hover over them. This physical position plus a haughty, preachy attitude will drive them away fast! And don't get your Bible out and just start nailing them. You need to be strong with your kids, but get on their level and speak to them with respect. Talk face to face. Be clear about what you believe, what you understand is going on, and what you expect from them. Treat them with respect and they will do the same to you.

## 2.   **They don't listen.**

Before you discipline, you must ask your young person for their side of the story. Give them a chance to accept responsibility for their actions or explain a possible misunderstanding. Ask them, "Tell me what you believe happened here, and I'll tell you what I know. Then we'll decide what to do."

### 3. They administer unjust punishment.

Think of the rebellion we would have in America today if every time we got a speeding ticket we were sentenced to five years in prison. An example of this with kids is when a parent grounds a kid for a year because they didn't pick up their room. Unjust punishment causes riots—in prisons and with kids. Make sure the punishment fits the crime.

### 4. They give them the silent treatment.

Parents can get so angry at their teenagers that they just refuse to talk to them. They freeze them out and reject them. This can be very hurtful and cause the teenager to draw further away from them in the long run.

### 5. They compare them to their other siblings.

"Why can't you do the dishes the way Jimmy or Sally does them? You are just as smart as your brother and sister, so why aren't your grades as high?" All this does is cause strife and jealousy between siblings, bringing more trouble into the family. Kids like to be treated as God sees them: unique individuals.

**6.      They take out their bad moods on them.**

If you had a bad day at the office and your boss didn't treat you right, Johnny or Janey shouldn't have to pay for your employer's lack of integrity. When things in your life get tough, you need to pray and get help from your spouse, Christian friends, or a pastor—then discipline your teenager. If the problem is something you can share with your young person, then do it. Ask them to pray for you. You build their confidence and self-esteem by sharing your life with them. The important thing is to keep your problems from creating more problems between you and your kids.

**7.      They never mention the Word of God
         or pray.**

The worst thing we can do to a teenager is to correct them and discipline them without giving them a biblical reason. It's so important that they see that our correction isn't just what we want but is based upon God's principles and wisdom. Then, if they want to argue, they will have to argue with Him! Also, if we pray for them and with them, taking them and their concerns to the Lord, He can soften their hearts and minds toward His Word.

Just remember that young people may act like they wish you lived on a different planet, but they really want your guidance and direction when it comes to their spiritual lives. They also want your correction and discipline when it comes to their natural lives. Be there for them and train them, take an active interest in them, give them God's Word whenever you can, and see if they are blessed and become the envy of their world.

# 6 Careers Your Teen Can Start Right Now[5]

1.   Newspaper business. Throw a paper route, write articles on community happenings and submit them to local publications, or start or contribute to a school paper.

2.   Investment broker. There are companies that will take investment capital of just $50. They can learn how the market works and start investing a little at a time.

3.   Graphic arts. If they have a bent for drawing and art, offer your assistance to find a place to use their gift. Some kids are already designing logos and Web sites for companies and churches.

4.   Film and video production. With an inexpensive camera and some software, they can be in the movie biz and produce projects or record school games and contests.

5. Lawn care. If you have a mower and a weed-eater, have them distribute flyers in their neighborhood and sign up accounts to cut and trim grass after school and all summer.

6. Child care. Encourage them to get certified from the Red Cross or another organization. Then help pass the word that they are available to families for quality baby-sitting services.

> >

Teenagers complain
there's nothing to do, then
stay out all night doing it.

Bob Phillips

Seven

# "Quit saying no and give me an alternative."

There is nothing worse to a teenager than being told no—and nothing else is said. When this happens, they feel like they have just been shut down with no place to go and nothing to do. "No" has placed them in a vacuum, wondering what to do next. You can show your teenagers that you really care about them by offering viable alternatives to sin and to the world's idea of fulfillment and pleasure. This will make you a hero in their eyes. God never just tells us no. He always gives us an alternative.

Therefore do not be unwise, but understand what the will of the Lord is. And do not be drunk with wine, in which is dissipation; but be filled with the Spirit, speaking to one another in psalms and hymns and spiritual songs, singing and making melody in your heart to the Lord, giving thanks

117

always for all things to God the Father in the name of our Lord Jesus Christ, submitting to one another in the fear of God.

Ephesians 5:17-21

God gives us lots of stuff to do instead of sinning and messing up. He says, "Listen, I've got something better for you. You don't need this false high of drugs and alcohol that the world offers. You can be filled with the power of the Holy Spirit. You can enjoy having the Spirit of God inside of you—and He won't give you a hangover! Instead, He'll give you joy unspeakable and full of glory. He'll show you which direction to take and give you wisdom to get where He's called you to go."

> >

**Your kids need to know that when they live for God— developing Christlike character and behavior—their lives are going to be so much better.**

"Just say no" has become an American catch phrase, but it's not God's way of doing things. That's why just saying no to our kids backfires on us. All it does is frustrate them and make them angry.

Fathers, do not irritate and provoke your children to anger [do not exasperate them to resentment], but rear them

118

[tenderly] in the training and discipline and the counsel and admonition of the Lord.

Ephesians 6:4 AMP

God says, "I want you to help your kids. Don't make them mad by just saying no. Admonish them, give them counsel, provide direction, train them. Give them things to do and instructions on how to do them in a wise and godly way—and make it interesting and fun if possible." Let's talk about three different scenarios that a lot of parents deal with and discuss some alternatives we could provide.

## Alternatives to Rebellion and Bad Attitudes

How do you handle worldly attitudes and rebellion in your kids? Do you tell them, "Stop acting that way," "I don't want you doing that," or "Change your attitude"? Obviously, they need to be told that their attitude and behavior are not acceptable to God, but we also need to tell them about the benefits of being Christlike instead. They need to see the good things that can happen when they make the right decisions and keep a good attitude.

Your kids need to know that when they live for God—developing Christlike character and behavior—their lives are going to be so much better. They're going to enjoy life more. They're going to have better relationships. One day they're going to have a better marriage.

119

They're going to have a better job. They're going to go further in life. They're going to have more success. They will sleep in peace at night and walk in peace during the day. Everything is better when you serve God and have a Christlike attitude.

A good passage of Scripture to read to them is Deuteronomy 28. In the first part of the chapter God declares all the blessings that believers walk in when they love and serve Him with their whole hearts. In the second part of the chapter He names all the curses that come upon those who reject Him or turn away from Him. Read these with your teenager and relate the blessings and the curses to what's going on in the world today. It's not hard to see that walking by God's Word and His Spirit is the best way to live.

You also need to tell your kids that even the world is discovering and recognizing what God says in Deuteronomy 28. There were some interesting studies done by the National Center for Addiction and Substance Abuse. They compared young people who had a deep faith in Jesus Christ or who seriously practiced a religion to teenagers who downplay faith, religion, and spirituality. They concluded that those who did not practice their religion were three times more likely to drink, to binge drink, and to smoke. They were four times more likely to use marijuana and seven times more likely to use illicit drugs.

They also found that those teenagers who attended religious services weekly also did much better. The kids who never attended services were twice as likely to drink and to smoke, three times as likely to use marijuana and binge drink, and four times more likely to use illicit drugs—all of which could not only shorten their lives but also make their lives difficult and miserable.

Our kids need to know that if they fool around with these things, they will develop addictions to them, and addition leads to terrible misery in life. If they marry, their relationship will be difficult. Their kids will be adversely affected by the addiction, and holding a job—not to mention succeeding at it and enjoying it—will be next to impossible.

These facts and statistics reinforce the wisdom of living for Jesus Christ instead of living for ourselves and according to the world's standards. Kids can easily see how much better their lives will be when they live for God. They can also see the privilege and honor of serving Him in this world. It's not that you have to—you get to! It is a tremendous adventure to live a life of faith in God and to do great exploits for Him.

Years ago a woman did a news report on Oneighty for the CBS *Early Show.* After we did the segment, she said, "You know,

> >

**Would you want to get up on Sunday morning if you heard your father or mother yell, "Come on! Get up! We have to go to church!"?**

ever since I filed that report I've never been able to stop thinking about the impact that you were having with kids. It made a serious impact on my life and how I'm raising my fourteen-year-old daughter." We sent her a Oneighty worship CD for background music to the piece, and she called and said, "There's power in that music. It's really good!"

Even the world sits up and takes notice when you are making a difference in kids' lives. And we need to communicate the blessings of being a Christian and being part of a Christian community to our own kids so that they will never take their faith and their relationship with God and His people for granted.

We often take for granted what we have in our church families and Christian communities here in America. We have the freedom to worship God as the Holy Spirit leads us without fear of torture or prison. But even more than that, we have a family of believers who are there to pray for us, believe with us, intercede for us, encourage us, inspire us, feed us the Word of God, and be those friends who stick closer than our natural siblings. When we take this great blessing for granted, our kids will too. We need to remind them more often that they are loved by God, by us, and by their church family.

If you're excited about your relationship with Jesus Christ, then your kids are going to be excited about their relationship with Him. If you're excited about going to services—hearing and learning the Word, experiencing the presence of the Holy Spirit, and fellowshipping with other believers—then your kids are going to be excited also. They're going to take their cues from you.

Would you want to get up on Sunday morning if you heard your father or mother yell, "Come on! Get up! We have to go to church!"? I don't think so, especially if you never had anything good to say about your relationship with God the rest of the week. But if you are continuously living the adventure of faith with your kids, on Sunday morning when they hear, "Good morning! It's time to get up and see what God has to say to us today," they will more likely be excited about God themselves.

What all this boils down to is that if you are living and presenting God's way of thinking and behaving, when your kid gets a bad attitude or acts in a rebellious manner, it will stick out like a sore thumb. If your teenagers don't catch themselves and repent, all you have to do is show them God's Word and they will see it for themselves. It doesn't take long for a kid to recognize the fact that when they are living for God their life is blessed, and when they aren't it is miserable.

## Alternatives to Worldly Partying

Most kids love to party. They love to get together with a bunch of friends and not have any plan. They just want to see what happens—which means a lot of bad things can happen. God knew this when He told us that without a vision—or a plan—we perish. We don't want our kids going to an unsupervised party for that very reason.

One of the greatest things Christian parents and churches can do is network together to provide great parties for their kids. They need safe places to go where there are fun things to do. They are looking for places where they can invite unsaved friends from school or their neighborhood, knowing that it will be a great time and not just preaching. They also need times on Friday and Saturday nights where they can meet other Christian kids and have fun doing things that will not harm them in spirit, soul, or body.

There are so many things that parents can do. We've had dance competitions in our backyard. We've had movie nights. At one of our son's birthday parties, he decided to have a poetry competition. His friends came with a poem or song they had written. It was hilarious, and all the kids had a great time. Just providing a place for them to gather and being there in the background gives them the freedom to talk. You're there, but you're not keeping them from having fun.

## Alternatives to Worldly Entertainment

Many parents back off when it comes to today's music because they don't know anything about it. They say, "I don't know what's going on, and it changes all the time." Then there are Christians who got saved and decided never to go to movies again. Now they have teenagers, and they don't have a clue about what's going on in the movie industry.

Because these parents don't know anything about worldly entertainment, they just say no to everything. They hear that rap songs are nasty, so they declare that there will be no secular music. Then they hear how corrupt and perverse Hollywood is, so they forbid their kids from going to the movies with their friends. But there has to be a proper balance.

Unfortunately, one of the reasons that a lot of parents don't want to deal with the entertainment issue is that they don't want to put in the work to find out what's going on. They won't make the effort to sit down and listen to the CDs, find out what the lyrics are, and research what kind of person the artist is. They don't read movie reviews to find out what the movies are presenting and how they are presenting it.

You don't have to go buy the CD or pay to see the movie. You can get on the Internet and find out anything you want to know. If you don't

> >

**You can have a good dialogue with your kids about suitable entertainment and come to an understanding about what is acceptable to God and what is not acceptable to Him.**

have a computer, go to any bookstore or library and do the research. You can find the lyrics to any song that you want and even listen to it online. You can read reviews of movies and see the previews and trailers online even before they come out. The ratings tell you if there is violence, bad language, sexual content, and other things.

When your kids want to get a certain CD or see a certain movie, ask them if they know about it. Tell them you want to look it up and do some research beforehand, and then share your findings with them. You can have a good dialogue with your kids about suitable entertainment and come to an understanding about what is acceptable to God and what is not acceptable to Him.

I've had parents tell me, "I'll only let my kid watch Christian movies, listen to Christian music, and read Christian magazines and books because that's all Jesus would do." I just remind them that there was no contemporary Christian music, books, movies, and videos in Jesus' time. And Jesus was known to visit and eat with "publicans and sinners." He didn't do this every day and He never compromised who He was, but He was not totally insulated from the secular culture of His day.

The key to this is wisdom and knowledge. First, you find out the content of the book or movie or CD. Then you make a decision on whether it is appropriate for your kids. For example, *The Passion of the Christ,* produced and directed by Mel Gibson, was a great film about Jesus. However, it might be too graphic for your kids if they are only five or six years old. On the other hand, there might be a good secular movie that has a great life-message, which would be extremely appropriate for an older teenager.

The point is, we don't throw caution to the wind and let our kids be exposed to anything or take their word for it when they say that something is okay. But we don't just say no to everything and just sit on our hands either. We educate ourselves about the entertainment industry and then take the time to educate our kids. In the end, we realize that entertainment is just another opportunity for us to share God's Word with our kids in bite-size pieces like we talked about in the last chapter.

I've observed those Christian young people whose parents separate them from the world almost completely. Their lives are centered totally around their church and their church school. They have no activities other than those related to the Christian community. Some even go to a Christian college. It's like they are in a vacuum where they never even smell the world. They hardly know the world exists out there. They've never heard or seen anything worldly. They only talk to an unbeliever when they go to the store to buy something.

Some of these kids go to a college or university that isn't Christian or start working in a secular company when they are eighteen to twenty-one years old and the world just overwhelms them. They have no idea

> >

One of the best things you can do for your kids is put them to work as soon as they are old enough. It makes them feel important, builds self-esteem and confidence, and teaches them responsibility and teamwork. It lets them know that they are not on this earth alone, and everyone has to do their part.

how to deal with it, and depending on their personality, they either get sucked right into the world in an effort to fit in or they become so rigid that no one can get along with them. Neither one of these scenarios is a good one!

Part of training up our kids is allowing them to learn how to live in the real world as they are ready so they can make right choices while we are still there to help guide them. They need to learn how to discern what is godly, what I call "value neutral" (neither good or bad—like which flavor of ice cream they choose), and what is evil. They need to learn how to make good decisions in difficult situations. How can they learn to choose God's way over the world's way if we completely insulate them from any contact with the culture they are living in?

God's plan is for your kids to interact with their world wisely while they are under your care and instruction. And if they do make an occasional mistake, you are there to love them, give them God's Word, and point out that they have just proved His Word to be true! There are some kids who choose to learn that the hard way. They want to touch the hot stove to make certain it really will burn them. It's better for them to learn that in your home, before they are out on their own. Then, by the time they are adults, they will know from personal experience that it is better to live by God's principles than by the ways of the world.

## Put Them To Work

One of the greatest alternatives to just saying no is giving your kids a job to do, finding them a job outside your home, or making them get a part-time job. Many teenagers believe that work is evil, but Adam and Eve worked before sin, death, and misery came into the picture. So we know that work is not a dirty, four-letter word. God gave us work to give us pleasure and satisfaction in our lives.

The importance of work is something every kid needs to know if they are going to succeed in life and enjoy it, but especially Christian kids. Christian teenagers ought to be excited about what God has called them to do, knowing that everything He has them accomplish is for a higher good and purpose. Parents should teach them from an early age that even the trivial tasks and unpleasant jobs they do as kids are part of God's plan for their lives. Nothing they do is insignificant.

One of the best things you can do for your kids is put them to work as soon as they are old enough. It makes them feel important, builds self-esteem and confidence, and teaches them responsibility and teamwork. It lets them know that they are not on this earth alone, and everyone has to do their part.

There's something important you need to know about putting teenagers to work, however. Most of them despise hard work! You may think that if you've got a good kid, they're just going to love work, that they will look forward to getting up early in the morning and doing some manual labor. But that is rarely the case, and sometimes parents get discouraged because their kids don't like to do chores or go to their part-time jobs.

I want you to know that it is very natural for teenagers—even those who are good kids and love God—to not enjoy flipping hamburgers or cleaning the garage. But then, we all have to overcome this, don't we?

> Do not love sleep lest ye come to poverty, open your eyes and you will be satisfied with bread.
>
> Proverbs 20:13

God knew that all human beings had a problem with work, and that is why the Bible, and particularly the book of Proverbs, is filled with admonitions to work hard. We're instructed to avoid laziness, slothfulness, oversleeping, and procrastination because He knows that we have trouble in this area.

> If anyone will not work, neither shall he eat. For we hear that there are some who walk among you in a disorderly manner, not working at all, but are busy-bodies. Now those who are such we command and exhort through our Lord Jesus Christ that they work in quietness and eat their own bread.
>
> 2 Thessalonians 3:10-12

131

Notice that the Bible tells us that when we don't work, we shouldn't eat! Parents need to teach their kids that without sowing they will not reap, and many of their opportunities in life happen because they get up and get busy. Every now and then God will bless them with something right out of the blue, but in most cases they will have to work for their reward.

These verses also say that when we don't work, we become disorderly and begin to stick our noses into everyone else's business. In other words, we stop taking responsibility for our own lives and start pointing our finger at everyone else. Bad attitudes emerge more easily when we are not doing something we should be doing. When you put your kids to work, you are not only teaching them many valuable lessons in life, you are also keeping them out of trouble!

Let me put your heart at ease that just because a kid appears to be lazy or doesn't like to work, it doesn't mean that they are not going to turn out right! Every human being has to come to grips with work, and some people never do. But believers have an understanding of work that the world doesn't, and this is what you need to teach your kids.

Work is a form of worshipping God. Your kids are not just cleaning the gutters or weeding the garden; they are being good stewards of all God has given, honoring their mother and father by obeying them, and learning patience, perseverance, and endurance. If they are doing the job with others, they are learning how to bear one another's burdens and prefer

>>

Every kid wants a mission impossible! They long for an epic battle, to be a hero in the fight of good versus evil, to see God make a way where there is no way—and use them to do it.

others before themselves. Work is a great teacher of God's Word.

The world looks at work as a curse, but God gave work as a blessing. We need to start teaching our kids this from the time they are little, and when they are teenagers their work can be even more significant. They might find a part-time job in a business they will run someday!

Here are some principles to help you in putting your teenagers to work:

1.  Don't overdo it. Make sure they are not working too hard or too much. They are still kids!

2.  Show them how to do it right. If they are working for you, you need to give clear instructions and train them before you turn the job over to them. If you fail to do this, you will provoke them to anger and frustrate them.

3.  Inspect their work. If they are doing a job for you, make sure you check it. This shows them that their work is important to you and gives you the opportunity to fine-tune your instructions and training. If they don't work for you, have a chat with their boss now and then to see how they're doing. Remember that you will answer to God for their training, not their boss.

4.  Praise them and thank them along the way. Nothing keeps a worker more inspired and

motivated than praise and thanks. You don't want them to feel like you're taking advantage of them or just using them. You want them to know that you value them and their good work.

5. Reward them. If they do an excellent job, give them something extra than what was promised. Even if they are getting a paycheck from someone else, it means a lot to them when you find some way to show them how proud you are of their achievements.

One last thing about work. Working with your teenagers is a great experience for you and for them. When I work with my boys out in the yard on a Saturday and we're pulling weeds or mowing grass, we may not say a whole lot, but we're accomplishing something together. We share the satisfaction of a job well done at the end of the day. And, of course, they always enjoy it and it's fun for me to give them all some cash! In the end, work is not so bad and they begin to understand the pleasure God gives in it.

## Mission Impossible

I love the story of Shadrach, Meshach, and Abednego. They were Jewish kids who were taken captive and found themselves in the middle of worldly Babylon—but they had values. They were living for God and knew what they believed. They had been taught how to pray and to trust God. They were also very bright and good workers, so the king used them to serve him.

Everything was going along real well until the king built a statue of himself and commanded his subjects to worship him while listening to some nice, worldly music. Although the boys were young, they had been trained in the ways of the Lord. They knew that their lives would lose God's blessing if they worshipped anyone other than Him. They said, "We're not going to bow."

Shadrach, Meshach, and Abednego were in the world but not of the world. They illustrated God's plan for our young people. First, He wants to save them and get them out of the world. Then He wants them to be discipled and trained by us to get the world out of them. Finally, He wants to put them into the world where they can have influence and make a difference in people's lives, to impact their culture for Jesus Christ.

Every kid wants a mission impossible! They long for an epic battle, to be a hero in the fight of good versus evil, to see God make a way where there is no way—and use them to do it. So don't just say no to your kids. Educate them and train them so they can see that serving Jesus Christ is the greatest adventure—and fun—on earth.

# 6 Reasons To Teach Your Teen To Say No to Premarital Sex[1]

1.  They will keep the door closed on the sin of sexual immorality and its destructive nature.

2.  The thought of raising a baby while they're a teenager will never have to enter their mind [or yours!].

3.  They will never have a doctor tell them that they've contracted a sexually transmitted disease—or worse, that they have HIV or AIDS.

4.  Friends and classmates will never see compromise in their life, which would cause them to talk behind their back and lose respect for who they are.

5.  God will be able to trust them with His very best as they give Him their very best.

6.    They will never have to deal with "ghosts of relationships past" in their marriage relationship.

> >

Thank God I had two
parents who loved me enough to
stay on my case.

Shaquille O'Neal

Eight

# "Don't let my friends be the first to tell me about sex."

Believe it or not, your kids want you to have the sex talk with them. Not only that, they want you to do it early enough so that when their friends start talking about it, they will know what they're talking about—and maybe know more than their friends know. It's embarrassing for them to discover this whole issue of sexuality from their friends, to not know about it when their friends do.

My own experience was something like that, and I'll never forget how embarrassed I was that my friends knew about sex and I didn't. In those days and in my family you just didn't talk about such things. I will also never forget when my dad finally decided he needed to tell me about it—I was sixteen.

He said, "Blaine, I just want you to know, if you're ever with a girl, don't do it. But if you do do it, use protection."

That was it! That was my parental instruction on sex and purity. He didn't know any better, and I didn't either. No one in my family was saved yet, and that was world's idea of the "sex talk." Nevertheless, we both knew something was wrong. After my family and I were saved, we learned God's way of going about educating kids about sex.

> >

**The only hope kids have is their parents or an adult who will take the time to tell them God's truth and make them accountable for it.**

People perish without the knowledge of God. If we don't want our kids to fall into sexual sin, we need to teach them biblical purity and values when it comes to relationships with the opposite sex. Then they won't be embarrassed with their friends when the subject comes up, and they will make the right decisions.

## The Least Influence

According to the latest statistics, 29 percent of all teenagers find out about sex from their friends, 16 percent learn about it from other places such as in their school's sex education classes or from their coaches and teachers, and 5 percent learn from other siblings and relatives. Most of what kids learn about sex is outside of their home. In other words, parents have the least influence on their kids when it comes to sex.

It is interesting to me that Madonna, who has probably done more to bring sexual content into media than any other celebrity in the last twenty years, has completely changed her position since she became a mother and a proponent of Kabala, which is a mystic religion based on Jewish writings. She is now determined to be the only influence on her children when it comes to sex. With regard to her six-year-old daughter, she said, "I want to protect her from sex. Full stop. She's not aware of sex nor should she be."

Madonna saying she will shield her daughter from the awareness of sex is like Bill Gates saying he will stop his kids from using a computer! But it's not easy for any of us. The world we live in, especially in America, is saturated with sexual content. Sex is in movies, television, commercials, on billboards, in magazines, music videos, and books—even "classics" in the public library. You can't drive through town or skim a magazine in a waiting room without encountering sexual images.

The only hope kids have is their parents or an adult who will take the time to tell them God's truth and make them accountable for it. So how does a parent go from being the least influence to the greatest influence? You have to take the time and make the effort to educate your kids on what God's truth is about sex, then discuss how they apply that truth in their daily lives, especially in the modern American dating scene.

## The Shopping Cart

What they need to know really comes down to two issues:

1.  Who they choose in a romantic relationship.

2.  What they do with the person in that relationship.

Concerning the first issue, you should never have a "shopping cart" mentality when it comes to dating. Have you ever been really hungry, gone into the grocery store, grabbed a cart, and just gone down the aisles picking up anything that looked good? The trouble with that method is that when you get to the checkout counter, your bill is usually a lot more than you had budgeted, you have a lot of stuff that you don't need—and most of it is junk food that isn't good for you.

That's the way it is with teenagers. Without a solid and fulfilling relationship with Jesus and their parents and family, they get so hungry for a meaningful relationship that they will go to the mall with their friends and latch onto the first person who looks good to them. They will take anything that comes along. And the result is usually heartbreak and disaster.

In order to get our kids to the marriage checkout stand in a healthy, godly condition, we need to give them some instruction on how to be discerning and wise in choosing who they will date and marry. First of all, you don't go to the grocery store without a list. And the list involves healthy, good food that will bless your body and not destroy it. The same is true in relationships. We study the Word of God because it contains our list—all the qualities and wisdom we need to discern people and have healthy relationships.

> >

**Help your kids focus on discovering who they are and who God called them to be instead of focusing on who they want to be with.**

Then you've got to pick a good cart. Have you ever gotten one of those shopping carts with a bad wheel or two that squeaks and swerves and you're constantly wrestling with it to make it go in the right direction? No matter how hard you try to keep it on course, it just veers to the right or left without warning. Because a shopping cart has four wheels, I want to give you four things to pass on to your kids to keep their dating cart accurate.

## 1.    Know Jesus.

If you don't know and love Jesus, having a daily relationship with Him, the rest of your relationships will suffer. Matthew 6:33 says that if you seek God's kingdom first, everything else you need in life will come to you. So you've got to put Jesus before any other relationship in order for the rest of your relationships to be on track.

When you put Jesus first and have a good relationship with Him, it keeps you from becoming desperate. Christian young people can get so desperate. I hear them say, "My friends are all dating. I've got to find somebody. I've got to be hooked up. I was hooked up last week, but I'm not hooked up this week. Who do I hook up with?"

The devil sits on their shoulders and tells them that there won't be anyone left for them at the end of the day. All single men and women will be taken by the time they are ready to get married! And the only thing that overcomes these lies is the truth of God's Word. Jeremiah 29:11 says that God has a plan and purpose for their lives that is good, and in Genesis 2:18 God Himself says that it isn't good for man to be alone. That means that He has a mate for them.

Tell your kids to look at those they know who have recently made it to the checkout stand, young adults who are a few years older than they are and are getting married or have gotten married. Point out that they come in all shapes and sizes and still found their mate and got married. There's hope for everyone! They don't have to get desperate and load up their cart with food that is bad for them. They can trust God, stay pure, and wait for the one He has for them because their relationship with Him is strong. They know that He orders their steps and will bless them at the right time and with the right person.

## 2.    Know yourself.

Help your kids focus on discovering who they are and who God called them to be instead of focusing on who they want to be with. Instead of thinking about who they can get or who they can go out with, encourage them to think about what they should be doing and where they are going in life.

The most important discovery to make when you're young is not who you want but who you are. God gives the teenage years to develop yourself, to build godly character, to understand your personhood—who you are in Christ—and to become a whole, healthy, purpose-filled individual. Then you will make good decisions for your life, particularly when it comes to choosing a mate.

Teenagers also have the drive and time to develop their gifts, talents, and abilities. This is when you try out all kinds of things that interest you and God shows you what you are called to do. Sadly, I have found that a lot of teenagers are wasting their time. When they could be developing their gifts and talents—practicing music or being coached in athletics or learning all about science—they are obsessed with dating and having romantic relationships.

147

Kids can get so busy and wrapped up in relationships that they forget to do what they are supposed to be doing: finding out who they are and what God has created them to do. Then it becomes a vicious cycle. They don't know who they are, so their romantic relationships end in pain and heartache. They go from one relationship to another, and as my wife pointed out one day, it is like they are practicing marriage and divorce over and over again. Then we wonder why it happens to them later on.

It's important to stress to your kids that their teenage years have a purpose, and that is to discover all God has for them. Why? Because only when they know who they are in Christ Jesus will they be able to recognize the mate He has for them.

## 3.    Cut out the word "love" in dating.

"I love you."

"I love you, too."

This is where the biggest problem in American dating lies: love is interchangeable with sex. This is the way it is portrayed in nearly every movie, TV show, music video, and magazine ad. Love and sex go hand in hand. "Well, if I love you, then it's okay to get physical." And that's where physical intimacy begins. They may start out holding hands, but then it progresses, one step at a time. Every time they go on a date they go a little bit further. And they believe it is okay because they love each other.

148

Kids should not be using the word "love" in a romantic way until they're either ready to give or to receive an engagement ring from someone they know is committed to them. This business of saying, "Mom, I'm in love with Susie," at age eleven is ridiculous. That word, in a romantic context, should be saved for when you are ready to be married. Why? If you think in terms of love, then you think in terms of all the things that go with love, including the physical things. And sex is for marriage only.

Let me tell you some well-known secrets. Boys have got turbo engines on their shopping carts! They are pushing as hard as they can to get to the checkout stand too early and too quickly. You need to talk about this with your boys and tell them to slow down. Trust God. Everything's going to be okay because He has the best plan.

A fifteen-year-old boy once said to me, "I finally found out what true love is. The only problem is, the girl that I'm in love with does not love me. I was wondering if you could help me out."

My answer was, "Leave her alone. If she doesn't want you, then you don't want her. If you are meant to be together, she'll come around. In the meantime, she's not interested, so let it go. Turn the whole thing over to God and go on with your life. There's somebody out there for you. You don't have to push it. You don't have to be in a hurry. First Corinthians 13 says that love is patient and doesn't demand its own way!"

Boys need to know that one of the ways to keep a dating relationship on the right track is to keep from saying, "I love you." Again, that is reserved for when you present her with an engagement ring.

Girls need to know about the boys' turbo engine. After a date or two, if some guy looks deep into your eyes and says, "Oh baby, I love you," that doesn't mean he loves you. That means he "lusts" you. You have something he wants, and he'll tell you whatever you want to hear so he can get there. And even if he is sincere, he is taking things too fast and leading you into dangerous territory. I'm going to say it again: "I love you" is only appropriate when he pulls out the engagement ring, and sex is reserved for after you are married.

When I say you should cut out the word "love," I'm speaking strictly of the dating vocabulary. I'm not talking about Christian love in general. I'm not referring to, "I love you with the love of the Lord," which is the unconditional love from God that we all have for other people. Kids at Oneighty are always telling each other and other people in the church that they love them. But I'm talking about pushing a dating relationship too far too soon by using the word "love" outside the context of marriage.

## 4.     Don't be alone together.

Here is a statistic that I'm going to give you from the Blaine Bartel Research Committee, taken from a personal study of over twenty years of working with

> >

**Drawing up a relationship covenant is a great way to establish boundaries and safeguard a dating relationship because kids have to state what they believe, what their intentions are, and bring their parents in to hold them accountable.**

teenagers. Are you ready? One hundred percent of teenage pregnancies and teenage sexual diseases are a direct result of two teenagers being alone. What does this tell us? Don't be alone on a date!

I'm not saying they can never be alone. There are times when they have to drive somewhere together. Just don't go parking. They shouldn't be at someone's home when the parents are gone. They shouldn't go into a bedroom by themselves unless they are working on a project together, the door is open, and the parents are nearby—listening closely! They have to be very careful about being alone because that's when kissing and hugging leads to other things.

Remind your kids that when they get married they will be alone all they like, and it will be great. Alone is good when you're married. But alone leads to sin when you are not married. It's just that simple.

## Boundaries Make Dating Safe

A couple at Oneighty told me one day that they had a relationship covenant while they were dating. They actually agreed to what the rules and boundaries would be in the relationship before they had their first date. I believe this is a great idea. This will definitely separate the men from the boys because if they can't discuss these issues with someone, they probably shouldn't be going out with them. In other words, they should choose someone who has the same faith and values that they have.

This couple wrote down what the "rules of engagement" were in their dating relationship. They considered a lot of issues. What do we do? What don't we do? Let's be clear on what are values are up front. Let's not go through a discovery process, finding out what we believe is right and wrong as we go along, because our emotions may weaken us and we might compromise what we believe. They even asked their parents to help them with it.

I'm going to call them Jimmy and Susie. Here's a little bit of what they wrote out.

### *What Jimmy and Susie can do:*

1.  We can hang out together, which includes seeing movies and going to restaurants or concerts.

2.  We can ride in the same vehicle together in order to go someplace.

3.  We can hold hands and put arms around shoulders.

4.  We can talk on the telephone.

5.  We can pray together.

### *What Jimmy and Susie cannot do:*

1.  We cannot hang out together late at night, which means after ten or eleven o'clock.

2.  We cannot have unnecessary physical contact like rubbing each other's back and cuddling. If it isn't something we would do with our brother or sister, we shouldn't do it.

3.  We cannot have prolonged time together. Too much time together causes the desire for physical contact to increase.

They included verses of Scripture that would guide their relationship, and then they both signed it with their parents witnessing it. This may seen extreme to you in today's culture, but the Bible says that we are not to be conformed to our culture. It is not our standard. The Word of God is our standard.

> And so, dear brothers and sisters, I plead with you to give your bodies to God. Let them be a living and holy sacrifice—the kind he will accept. When you think of what he has done for you, is this too much to ask?
>
> Don't copy the behavior and customs of this world, but let God transform you into a new person by changing the way you think. Then you will know what God wants you to do, and you will know how good and pleasing and perfect his will really is.
>
> Romans 12:2 NLT

Drawing up a relationship covenant is a great way to establish boundaries and safeguard a dating relationship because kids have to state what they believe, what their intentions are, and bring their parents in to hold them accountable. Overall, it is a great way to stay out of trouble.

## A Scriptural Boundary

A lot of kids ask me, "How far is too far? What can I do on a date if I really like someone? Can we hug? Can we kiss? What are the rules?"

When it comes to this issue, I just have one rule based upon one verse of Scripture.

> Now concerning the things of which you wrote to me: It is good for a man not to touch a woman.
>
> 1 Corinthians 7:1,2

Now before you accuse me of being too legalistic and strict, let's take a look at the word "touch." There are different kinds of touch in the Greek language. In this verse, the word "touch" is the Greek word *haptomai,* which means to attach oneself to, and the root word, *hapto,* literally means to set on fire or kindle.[1] So the

> > >
>
> **It has been found that you can change your teenager's sexual behavior by eating with them on a regular basis.**

apostle Paul is telling the single man that he should not touch a woman or fasten his body to hers in a way that would arouse her sexual desires.

A young man asked me, "Pastor Blaine, whenever I hold my girlfriend's hand, man, I'm getting excited. The passions, the fires, are stirring up. I'm thinking about the next thing. What do I do?"

I said, "Don't hold her hand. Tell her what's going on and she should understand. Just avoid it."

He said, "Well, how are people going to know we're together. No one will know. We've got to let people know we're together."

I said, "Whatever you have to do to stay pure, then do it. If someone doesn't get that you're together, you can tell them."

Someone said to me, "Kissing can't be that bad."

I said, "Have you ever been sexually aroused by a kiss?"

The Word of God makes it very clear to men and women of all ages just what the godly boundaries are for physical contact in dating. If sexual passion becomes aroused, you have crossed the line and are headed for trouble—and kissing certainly falls into that category.

In 1 Corinthians 16:20, Paul exhorts the entire body of Christ to "Greet one another with a *holy* kiss." The very fact that he brings this up tells us that there was a kind of kiss that did not kindle the fires of passion in the opposite sex—and that there was a kiss that did. In many countries and cultures today, people will greet each other by kissing on the cheek and some-times on the lips. This is what Paul was referring to as a "holy" kiss. He was making a distinction between a holy kiss and a kiss of passion.

Touch is how you go from being okay to entering dangerous territory sexually, so it is an important subject to discuss with your teenager. It takes guts to sit down and have that dialogue with your kid, to say, "Hey, let's talk about this. I know it's embarrassing, but let's just get it out on the table, so that I know that you have a thorough understanding of what you are dealing with here."

## Tell Them When They Are Young

In order for your kids to know about sex from you instead of their friends, you have to talk to them as soon as they are old enough to understand the physi-ology of it. They will probably be grossed out, but assure them that it's okay. They're supposed to be grossed out at that age! Let them know that this is a subject you will be discussing with them as they grow older and have questions. In other words, your door is always open. Also, tell them that when they meet their mate and get married, it will be one of the greatest blessings of their life. This gives them the facts, let's them know their present reaction is normal, and lays the foundation that God created sex to be a great pleasure between a husband and wife.

Here's the point. The world attempts to portray sex in an immoral way even to our children. They've been out front and unashamed in actually selling this to our teenagers. On the other hand, many parents and even Christian parents and the Church have been relatively silent on this issue. As a result, we're not giving our young people a fighting chance to make it through the battlefield without falling and becoming a casualty.

> >

**To communicate well, you have to have a grasp of the world your kid is facing. It is entirely different from the world you faced as a teenager.**

We've got to arm our kids with the truth. It is our responsibility to help them to know what is right and what to do. Kids are finding out about sex at younger ages today, so the sooner you tell them what you believe, the better equipped they will be. When my first son was five years old, I came home from work and before I could say hello he asked, "Daddy, what's sex?"

I thought, *Man, what is going on?* Is my son a pervert? I said, "Hold on, Son." I ran to Cathy and said, "Honey, what's going on with Jeremy? How come he's asking me what sex is?"

She said, "Well, I was in the greeting card section of the store today, and he found this card that had those three letters on it. He sounded it out just like they've been teaching him in phonics. Once he figured it out, he said, 'Sex. Mommy, what's sex?' And I told him that you would tell him when you got home."

I was then confronted with the reality that it was my job to explain to a five-year-old what sex was. And that was not easy. "Well, you know, it's when Mom and Dad kind of show love and affection and hugging and embracing and stuff."

He said, "Well, that's cool. Kind of like what you and I do when you give me a hug when you drop me off at kindergarten?"

I said, "No, no, no! Not like that."

## Sex Is Not a Four-Letter Word

It doesn't get easier to talk about sex when they are older. There is really no easy way to talk to your teenager about sex. It's awkward in the beginning, but these kinds of discussions are what make the difference in your relationship—and in their ability to stay strong and pure. It's what makes you a "hands on" parent who is involved in your kids' lives. I suggest praying in tongues for three hours to get up your courage!

Before you talk to them, know what you're talking about. Read books like this one. Be well prepared. And when you do sit down to talk, make it a conversation instead of a lecture. I've done this with my boys individually and together, and I always open it up to hear what they are seeing, hearing, and thinking as well as what I want to get across to them. We always end up learning from each other.

You could also read a book together. One of the best-selling books on teenage relationships is called *I Kissed Dating Good-bye,* by Joshua Harris. He wrote the book when he was still a teenager. If you read through something like that together, discussing a chapter at a time, you will easily get into all the things you want to talk about with your kids.

This is going to sound strange, but it has been found that you can change your teenager's sexual behavior by eating with them on a regular basis. It is disturbing that, according to a YMCA survey, 10 percent of the parents surveyed reported that they ate just one meal a week or never ate with their teenagers. They found that 50 percent of teenagers who do not eat dinner with their parents have had sex by age fifteen. By contrast, only 32 percent of teenagers who eat dinner with their parents regularly have ever had sex.

Seven out of ten young people who regularly eat and talk with their parents do not have sexual relations before they get married.[2] That says that we need to be sitting down to dinner with our kids!

## Know Their World

To communicate well, you have to have a grasp of the world your kid is facing. It is entirely different from the world you faced as a teenager. At Oneighty we subscribe to *Rolling Stone* magazine to keep up on what kids are listening to and looking at. We want to know what they're involved in and what the entertainment industry is saying to them.

One day I was flipping through one of the recent issues and saw an ad for an antiperspirant and was struck by the sexual content. A few pages later there was a picture of Angelina Jolie, who was talking about sex in the quotes at the top. When I turned the page I saw what she was selling—a car. Even advertisements are selling products with sexual images.

The American Psychological Association estimates that teenagers are exposed to fourteen thousand sexual images, references, and innuendoes per year on television. A 2001 study of prime time television by the Kaiser Family Foundation found out that 75 percent of TV programs today include sexual content of some kind. It's almost impossible to find anything on TV that is not offensive in this area.

> Flee also youthful lusts; but pursue righteousness, faith, love, peace with those who call on the Lord out of a pure heart.
>
> 2 Timothy 2:22

In this verse of Scripture, the apostle Paul tells Timothy to flee youthful lusts. We don't know how old Timothy was, but he was much younger than Paul. He was also the pastor of the church at Ephesus. Paul had to command and encourage this young minister of the gospel to flee the lusts of his youth. If a young man like Timothy, who loved God with all his heart, needed that admonition, how much more does every Christian teenager in America need to hear it?

Paul doesn't stop there, though. He says, "But pursue righteousness, faith, love, peace, with those who call on the Lord out of a pure heart." This is so important! To help our young people escape the trap of youthful lusts and pursue righteousness, faith, love, and peace, they need to be surrounded by those who call on God with a pure heart.

Your kids can't do it alone, and they know it. They need your help and guidance. They need help from those who understand that they are not just your child but God's precious child. And I believe that involves all of us in the Church. We have a responsibility not only to train our own kids, but to be a good influence and example to all young people.

# 3 Ways To Encourage Your Teen To Win Your Trust[3]

1.  Tell your kids that obeying you immediately, whether they feel like it or not, makes you trust them.

2.  Tell your kids that when they honor you when you speak to them, it makes you trust them.

3.  Tell your kids that when they are truthful, even when it gets them in trouble, it makes you trust them.

>>

The best way to keep
children at home is to make
the home atmosphere
pleasant, and to take the air
out of the tires.

Dorothy Parker

Nine

# "My parents don't trust me."

This is something your teenagers tell me a lot, especially when it comes to sex and dating issues. A fourteen-year-old girl wrote to me, "I have a boyfriend that I've been dating for three months. We love each other very much, and my parents don't trust me, and I want them to trust me so much. I have very big morals, and I won't have sex until I'm married. What can I say or do to get their trust?"

How many times have you heard, "You don't trust me"? It's probably not that this fourteen-year-old girl's parents don't trust her as much as they don't trust everything and everybody else: the dating process, the world in which she dates young men, and especially the teenage boys she goes out with!

I believe the American dating process is flawed. The way it is now is a set-up for moral failure and a dry run for marriage and divorce. I'm not condemning those who

> > >

**How can a parent trust their kid? There has got to be clear and frequent communication between you. You can't just "lay down the law" and let them go out the door, expecting them to do what you've told them to do.**

do believe in the dating process, but I want to throw out some ideas for your consideration.

Right now the dating process in America works like this. Two young people see each other. They're physically attracted to each other. They like each other. Many times, especially when they're younger, their initial contact will be to send messengers to each other. These messengers are young people, usually, who don't have dates themselves, but they can be a part of the process in helping to hook up others.

The messenger will say, "Hey, Jerry, did you know that Sally likes you?"

"Oh, really? Well, I didn't know that. But I'm happy to know that because I like her."

Now Jerry is bold enough to go up to Sally and say, "Hey, would you go out with me?" Or, today Sally might ask Jerry out! And the process begins.

They go out and they like each other even more. Then the relationship goes a step further. They commit to one another. "I'm committed to you. Are you committed to me?" When commitment is established, that's when the word "love" gets thrown around. And we have already discussed the problem with that. Today most teenagers believe that love and sex go together, so their physical intimacy will usually progress until they have sex.

My question is, "How can young Christians participate in this dating process and remain pure?" Consider the fourteen-year-old girl who wrote me about her parents not trusting her. Most likely she has years of dating ahead of her before she marries. If she's so involved with the issue of sex at fourteen, and she believes she is in love now, how will she remain pure until she marries?

Let me put it another way. If she will not marry until she's twenty, then she has six years of dating and trying to remain pure. Six years translates into 312 weekends, which is about 630 weekend nights and over 5,600 hours of being alone. That's a tough challenge for anyone, but especially a young person whose hormones are raging.

In light of all of this—the flaws in the process of dating and the youthful lusts that are present—how can a parent trust their kid? First of all, there has got to be clear and frequent communication between you. You can't just "lay down the law" and let them go out the door, expecting them to do what you've told them to do. You have to have an understanding between you that supports trust.

This brings us back to the sex talk. There is a time when kids are very young to have the sex talk with them. But as they grow up, you have little discussions as the opportunity presents itself. We saw in the last chapter that kids who have dinner with their parents regularly are less likely to be sexually active. This is not just because they're eating together, but because they are talking to one another about the issues of their lives. They are reaching an understanding of one another. Kids know what their parents expect and why, and they agree to follow the rules.

Then parents assure their kids that they will hold them accountable for the rules they have set for them and help them keep those rules. Their kids know that their parents have the right to investigate them, to make certain that they are keeping their end of the bargain.

What I'm talking about here is not easy to do. Even if your teenagers agree to the rules, situations will arise when they will try to bend the rules or break them altogether. They may accuse you of all kinds of things before all is said and done—including not trusting them. But you just go back to the rules, point out the biblical standards the rules are based upon, and stick with God's Word. Remind them that trust is earned.

## To Be or Not To Be Hands-On

A lot of parents say, "I want to be a cool parent. Man, I'm going to just let my kids grow up naturally.

170

I'm going to be hands-off. I'm going to let them do what they want, and they will like me a whole lot more." A study called the White House Conference found that not to be true. They discovered that most teens don't want to establish their own rules and expectations. They want their parents to be "hands-on" parents.

They found that 47 percent of teenagers living in a hands-on household had an excellent relationship with their fathers and 57 percent had an excellent relationship with their mothers. On the other hand, only 13 percent of teenagers with hands-off parents reported an excellent relationship with their fathers, and only 24 percent reported an excellent relationship with their mothers.

The more hands-on you are, the better your kids like it and the better your relationship will be. It makes sense that the more involved you are, the more you to talk to them, interact with them, and have fun with them. It's from spending time with someone and taking an interest in their life that you develop the inside jokes and close bonds in a relationship. Your kid is no exception, and this can develop mutual trust.

I like to think of it this way. When you are involved in your kid's life, you are honoring them. You are showing them that they are important and precious to you. Honor is a big deal to teenagers.

> >

It is harder to forgive ourselves than to forgive others, maybe because we get proud and think we are beyond sinning. Then when we do sin, we can't forgive ourselves. We have to help our teenagers understand that it's okay for them to forgive themselves.

Here are five ways to show H-O-N-O-R to your teenager:

H—How can I help you? Or, Can you help me with something?

O—Of all the kids I know, you're special.

N—Never hesitate to come to me. I'm here for you.

O—Okay, tell me what you think, then I'll tell you what I think.

R—Respect is earned and you can be rich. Show respect and you will be given respect.

Honor is shown by simply giving attention to a person, and teenagers crave attention! If you are having a hard time trusting your kid, consider how much attention you have been giving them. Have you honored your teenager lately by seeking their help, asking their opinion about a controversial issue, or simply spending time with them?

When you honor your young person, they will honor you and trust you; and they will have a great desire to please you and earn your trust.

## Trusting After a Fall

A sixteen-year-old girl e-mailed me, "I've made some very wrong decisions with my boyfriend. I just wish I'd never done what I did because I can't ever look at myself the way I was able to before. I wish I could go back in time, but I can't. What can I do?"

I believe the reason this girl was e-mailing me instead of talking to her parents was because she was afraid to go to her parents. Or maybe her parents aren't Christians. Either way, she needed help and didn't feel like she could go to them.

Most Christian kids who mess up, and kids who have been sexually active but then come to Oneighty and get saved, have a hard time getting over their past. They wish they could go back and erase it and do things differently. That's the first thing you have to understand when your teenager falls sexually. If you stand there and point your finger and condemn them, you will probably either crush their spirit or drive them right back into rebellion. Believe me, if they've grown up in the Word of God, they know they have sinned and are in big trouble.

After you assure them that God still loves them, you both need to go through the steps of forgiveness. Your teenager must ask God to forgive them for their sin and receive His forgiveness. Remind them that the Bible says in 1 John 1:9 that Jesus is faithful not only to forgive them, but to cleanse them from all unrighteousness. He will clean them up and make them pure again.

Then they need to forgive themselves. This is one of the hardest things for any individual. For some reason, the blood of Jesus seems good enough to cleanse everyone else but not us. It is harder to forgive ourselves than to forgive others, maybe because we get proud and think we are beyond sinning. Then when we do sin, we can't forgive ourselves.

We have to help our teenagers understand that it's okay for them to forgive themselves. In fact, they will only continue in pride by not forgiving themselves because they are setting themselves above God. He has forgiven them, so they should come into agreement with Him and His Word and forgive themselves too. In forgiving themselves, they are actively expressing their faith in a loving, heavenly Father by humbly doing what He has already done.

Finally, you need to forgive them and assure them of your love. This is often extremely difficult for a Christian parent. You are disappointed and heart-broken. Maybe you were careful to train your kid and they still messed up. Maybe you didn't train them and now you have just as many regrets about the past as your kid does. Either

> >

**There are a lot of concepts that are related to trust: responsibility, integrity, and a standard of excellence. You can't expect your teenager to earn your trust if you never give them guidelines and opportunities to earn it.**

way, what you thought would never happen has happened. You must forgive them, forgive yourself, and allow God to heal you as a family. Only He can make everything good and pure again.

When everyone has been reconciled to God and to each other, then you need to take care of the practical matters. Repentance means to decide to change and think differently.[1] When you think differently, you will act differently. You basically stop doing the wrong thing and start doing the right thing. So the first thing your young person must do is immediately terminate the relationship that brought them down. Cold turkey. They have to understand that they will never recover their passion for purity if they are continually fighting a passion for the person that caused them to sin. No matter how hard or painful, it must be done.

Second, from that moment on, your kid must be accountable to you or someone who also has a passion for purity. In the case of this young girl who e-mailed me, if she could not be accountable to her parents, she could turn to a spiritual counselor at church or a youth leader. But it must be someone who is stronger and more mature in the Lord. It also should be someone of the same sex.

## How To Earn Trust

There are a lot of concepts that are related to trust: responsibility, integrity, and a standard of excellence. You can't expect your teenager to earn your trust if you never give them guidelines and opportunities to earn it. Here are some guidelines I give my kids when they want to earn someone's trust.

1.  Do your job **better** than expected.

2.  Give attention to the smallest detail.

3.  Always finish what you start.

4.  Focus on the task that will produce the result; don't get so consumed with the result that you neglect doing the task in an excellent manner.

5.  Pay the price others may not pay. Be **extraordinary.**

Teach your teenager to do things with excellence because excellence builds trust. When they rake the leaves, they don't put the trash bags all over the yard; they put them neatly on the curb for the trash men to pick up. When they do the dishes after a meal, they not only wash and dry them, but they put them away where they belong. They wipe the countertops and sweep the floor so that the kitchen looks fresh and clean and ready to use again.

All these things are the little details of life that add up to being trusted. And this goes for dating and relationships as well. When they say they will be home at ten that night, they don't come in at five minutes after ten. They are home at ten or before ten. When they are interested in someone of the opposite sex, they tell you about

> >

**When we require our kids to live by God's Word, we are also teaching them to trust Him.**

them, have you meet them, and keep you "in the loop" as the relationship progresses. You get to know all their friends as they get to know them.

You need to tell your kids that earning trust is not always easy. I like to use the word "mediocre" to illustrate this point. Mediocre is formed from two Latin words: *medius* and *ocris. Medius* means middle or halfway, and *ocris* means a peak; sharp.[2] You could say that mediocre means, "halfway up a stony mountain." This implies that the road to the top is rough and you have given up halfway up. The dictionary says, "neither very good nor very bad; ordinary; average; not good enough; inferior."[3]

Sometimes earning someone's trust presents one of the biggest challenges. It's like climbing a stony mountain. You've gotten some nicks and some cuts and you're hurting and you want to quit. You have to scale some jagged rocks and push through some crevasses to keep going. Mediocrity stops halfway up and says, "You know, I'm too tired. They'll just have to be satisfied with what I've done so far. Someone else can finish, or I'll do it another time." But excellence pushes on until the summit is reached. Excellence pays the price to finish the job and do it well, and the reward of excellence is trust.

## Trust Is All About God

You can't hold your young person accountable and not give them the Word because the Word of God enables them to be trustworthy. Second Peter 1: 8 says that if the Word of God is in them and they are living by it (you are holding them accountable for it), they will succeed in life. By encouraging them in the Word and nurturing their relationship with the Lord, you can require them to be trustworthy because through Him they have the ability to be trustworthy.

Furthermore, there is only one way one human being can trust another human being, and that is by trusting God. It was only after her "close encounter" with God that Sarah was able to call Abraham "lord." (See Genesis 18:1-15 and 1 Peter 3:4-6.) She trusted Abraham by trusting the God of Abraham. We can only trust our kids by trusting their God and our God. We must remind ourselves that He has our kids' futures and our future securely in His hands.

When we require our kids to live by God's Word, we are also teaching them to trust Him. Without faith in God, it is impossible to please Him. (See Hebrews 11:6.) So our kids know that only through His strength and wisdom can they earn anyone's trust and favor. Without God, they can do nothing; but through Him all things are possible. (See Matthew 19:26.)

The only way a young person can go out and face the world with confidence is if they have earned trust during their growing up years. This means they have had to rely on God's strength to be trustworthy. As you train your teenager to earn your trust by relying on God's strength, you are building their own confidence in God to enable them to be trustworthy and responsible in the future.

If kids think they can't be trusted, they will never be trustworthy. But if they have proven time and time again that they can be trusted, they will have inner peace that with God's help they can meet whatever challenges and responsibilities life throws at them after they leave home.

As you require trustworthiness from them and put the Word in them, they come to understand that they can only trust themselves or anyone else to the degree that they trust God. He is the One who holds the keys to their success. He gave them their gifts. He has the plan for their lives. He leads them and guides them. He gives them the knowledge and wisdom they need for daily situations. And only He can give them the inner fortitude to keep them worthy of trust long after they have left your home and established their own.

# 5 Things You Must Teach Your Teen[4]

1.  How to live within their means.
    Challenge your teenager to delay
    instant gratification for true, long-term
    financial success.

2.  How to be happy with who they are.
    Don't allow your teenager to fall into
    the empty and vain comparison trap.
    Their happiness should be based on
    who they are in Christ and what He
    has created them to be and do.

3.  How to build a successful marriage.
    Have your teenager read books about
    building a marriage that will stand
    through the storms of life. Share the
    experiences you have had that can
    assist them.

4.  How to be a good parent. Most of us
    learn our parenting skills from how
    our parents raised us. As you grow as
    a parent, share your experiences and
    wisdom with your teenager.

5.   The meaning of life. The meaning of life can only be found in a personal relationship with our Creator. Teach your child from birth that the closer they are to Him, the closer they will be to fulfilling their life's purpose.

\> \>

When I was a boy of fourteen, my father was so ignorant, I could hardly stand to have the old man around. But when I got to be twenty-one, I was astonished at how much he had learned in only seven years.

Mark Twain

Ten

# "Be my friend—
# but don't tell anybody."

It's been my experience that if a troubled kid finds just one adult who will be their friend—and that means holding them to biblical standards and integrity—they can be turned around. For example, a young man I will call Kris came to our youth group, and he was having severe problems. He had threatened to kill other kids in his school and had created a list of those he was planning to murder, so he was expelled. Now he was coming to Oneighty on one of our buses on a regular basis.

I learned that his mother had given up on him. She was letting him do anything he wanted to do. His father was out of the picture altogether. One day one of my leaders came to me and said, "Blaine, we're concerned about this kid. He's violent and lashes out. What do you suggest we do?"

I said, "Bring him to my office next week." The following week I sat down with Kris before he came to our next Wednesday night service. I looked him straight in the eye and said, "Now, Kris, you are gonna smarten up. You're going to be a leader because you're not going to live this way anymore. You're going to quit lashing out and being a violent person, and you're going to be what God has called you to be."

He didn't say anything but I had his attention, so I continued. "It's time for you to grow up as a young man. I know you've had problems in your home, and I know that kids have made fun of you at school. But with Jesus in your life you're bigger than your problems at home or at school. You've been to Oneighty enough to know what we expect from you. From now on we are going to help you meet those expectations, and you are going to change the way you think, the way you behave, and the way you live."

No adult had ever leveled with him, challenged him, and given him direction. His face brightened, and I grabbed him by the hand to pray with him. It wasn't long before he was

> >

**Most kids want friendship with their parents to be their best kept secret! As a result, they don't make it a habit to ask you into their world. They want you to knock at their door.**

back in school and doing well. He's come to Oneighty every week since and has allowed Jesus to change his life. And all it took was a leader who took the time to sit down with him and say, "Hey, let's correct this behavior problem. Let's deal with this attitude that you've had."

If I could have that kind of impact with Kris, how much more can a parent have with their own kids? The kids I deal with love it when their parents treat them with respect and hold them to a scriptural standard of thinking and behavior. Why? Because they know they are loved. Then they become your best friends as they grow older.

## Keep Knocking on Their Door

As kids grow older they want to grow closer to their parents, but they don't often act like it. Just like the title of this chapter says, most kids want friendship with their parents to be their best kept secret! As a result, they don't make it a habit to ask you into their world. They want you to knock at their door.

Sometimes parents have the idea that if their kid is a really good kid, they're going to invite them to hang out with them, go to the movies with them, and come back to their bedroom to just talk for a while. But kids aren't like that. Inviting their parents to have fellowship with them does not come natural for kids. Generally they will not invite you into their world or seek you out, so you must ask to come in.

Proverbs 19:17 says, "A man who has friends must himself be friendly, but there is a friend who sticks closer than a brother." The Word of God tells us that to make friends, we must be friendly and reach out. This is critical to becoming a friend to a young person. They rarely just come to you, sit down, and open up their hearts, especially when they are dealing with something that is highly sensitive to them.

One of the ways you can get your teenager to open up is to ask questions and wait for answers. A lot of parents make the mistake of answering their own question. They don't give their son or daughter a chance to respond. Let them come out of their shell and talk to you. Sometimes you have to wait awhile to get them to give you more than a one-word grunt, but it is well worth the wait.

Another great way to get into your teenager's world is to do something that they like to do. Shoot baskets or play catch in the backyard. Go to the mall and do some shopping. Have lunch or dinner together. Take them to a concert or a movie, or go to the music store and listen to each other's favorite music.

What does it mean to keep knocking on their door? It means that you are making an effort to show them how important they are to you, that you not only love them because they are your kid but because you think they are a special person who is fun to be with and worth knowing. When you show that you care for them and like them that much, they will always consider you one of their best friends.

Let me demonstrate what I'm saying here. See if you can answer the following questions:

1. Name the five wealthiest people in the world this past year.

2. Name the last five Heisman trophy winners.

3. Name the last five winners of the Miss America contest.

4. Name the last five people who won the Nobel and Pulitzer prizes.

5. Name the last five academy award winners for best actor and best actress.

How did you do? Not so good? The point is, few people remember the headliners of yesterday. These are the best in their fields and yet we can't think of their names. Awards tarnish, achievements are forgotten, and accolades and certificates are buried with their owners when there is no real personal benefit.

> >

**The people who make a difference in your life are not the ones with the highest credentials, the most money, or the greatest rewards. They are the people who simply care about you.**

Now here's another quiz.

1.   List five teachers who helped you through school.

2.   Name five friends who helped you through difficult times.

3.   Name five people who have taught you something life-changing.

4.   Name five people who have made you feel appreciated.

5.   Name five people who are a lot of fun to be with.

Was this second quiz easier? Why? Because the people who make a difference in your life are not the ones with the highest credentials, the most money, or the greatest rewards. They are the people who simply care about you. Your best friends are the ones who value you and care about you—and so are your kids!

## What Kind of Friend Are You?

Caring for your kids by seeking them out, asking questions, and playing and working with them is great, but there are other aspects of being a good friend. They also need to know that you will be there for them through thick and thin. You will pray and seek God and do whatever needs to be done to see that they get their answer.

A friend loves through all kinds of weather, and families stick together in all kinds of trouble.

Proverbs 17:17 MESSAGE

A true friend is somebody who is there in the good times and the bad times, and who doesn't desert you in times of trouble. That's what we need to be to our kids—especially when they mess up in a big way and embarrass us! Yes, we straighten them out with discipline and instruction; but we also make it clear that we are sticking with them no matter what people say.

Friends are also honest with each other, even when they know it may offend or hurt.

Wounds from a friend can be trusted, but an enemy multiplies kisses.

Proverbs 27:6 NIV

Good friends tell each other the truth in love, and that's what parents should do for their kids. As they grow older they trust you more and more because they know you've always been honest with them. When they needed correction, you brought correction. When they stepped out of line or were about to step out of line, you made them deal with it. You weren't one of those "friends" who never confronted them when they were doing wrong or about to do the wrong thing.

Confronting sin, deception, mistakes, and errors in judgment is all part of being a good parent and a good friend. Your kids may not appreciate it now, but as they grow older and see how your guidance and care have saved them from a lot of misery and ruin, they will begin to welcome your advice and counsel as a friend.

# How To Be a Friend to Your Kid Now

As you deal with your teenagers, there is always this line between being the parent and being the friend. Because they are in that transitional phase between being a child and being an adult, your role has to be more flexible. There are times when you must be the one in authority, the disciplinarian, the teacher, and the one who holds them accountable. Then there are other times when you can be their friend and confidant—and they can be yours.

There are some things that I have learned mean a lot to them. Here are a few of the things you can do to develop a friendship with your teenager.

## 1.    Do not embarrass them in front of their friends.

Don't give them a big kiss in front of their friends as you drop them off at school. When you pick them up at a friend's house, don't walk in dressed sloppy and looking weird. Always consider their world and

> >

When you invest in your kid, you're making a significant contribution to their life and their future. Some may accuse you of spoiling your kids, but remember: things don't spoil a kid; giving them everything they want without requiring responsibility and character is spoiling a kid.

what might embarrass them when you are around their friends.

## 2.     Step into their world.

Your kids are in school all day, and you're not there with them. They are unique individuals and how they relate in their world is going to be unique. So ask them about their lives and then listen carefully and prayerfully to their answers.

Whether you enjoy the activities they enjoy or not, show an interest and support them. Go to their baseball games and music concerts. If they are in a rock band and play loud music you hate, go anyway and wear ear plugs! And surprise them on their own turf every now and then. Just show up at a football or cheerleading or band practice. Don't do this often, but just randomly enough to make sure they know you're interested in everything that concerns them.

## 3.     Help them think about and plan for
##          their future.

Some kids know what they want to do when they grow up from a really early age, and that makes it easier for you because you can help them prepare for it. But other kids scratch their heads and feel lost. It's not clear to them. So you can help them by just bringing it up every now and then. "Hey, have you got any ideas about what you'd like to do when you get out of school? Do you sense God leading you into a particular career or life calling?"

If they say no to those questions, you can say, "Well, let me ask you some questions. You may not know the answers, but you may not have thought about these things, and it'll just get you thinking about them. Where do you want to live? What are your gifts? What do you like to do? What do you see yourself doing as you get older?"

Take time to pray with them and say, "Let's pray that God will lead you. The Bible says that your steps are ordered of the Lord, so He knows where you're going. It also says that young people are arrows, and arrows need direction." And by the way, arrows don't get to where they're going by themselves. They are aimed and fired by someone—and that's you!

## 4. Help them get stuff they need—and don't need.

Kids are always asking for things. Sometimes they need the stuff and sometimes they don't. If they really want it, however, you can use that desire to teach them responsibility. Maybe they can work in the yard a few weekends or organize and do a garage sale for you in exchange for a certain percentage of the profits. Depending on the cost of what they want, they may want to get a part-time job. You can also pledge to contribute an amount to the cost if they maintain a certain grade average or keep their room clean and straight. This helps keep their focus on the things that matter, even if they are doing it to get something that won't really matter in the long run.

I guarantee that Bill Gates' parents are real happy that they got him a computer when he was fifteen years old. He used it to write some software for his city, which he sold to the city for $20,000. By the time he was eighteen, he and his partner were being paid a salary of $30,000 a year to write software and doing computer programming part-time, after school. His parents made an investment in his life that determined his destiny.

When you invest in your kid, you're making a significant contribution to their life and their future. Some may accuse you of spoiling your kids, but remember: things don't spoil a kid; giving them everything they want without requiring responsibility and character is spoiling a kid. I believe parents are called to be their kids' provider just as Father God provides for us all— and sometimes He blesses us with things we didn't earn just because He loves us and He knows we can handle the responsibility.

Galatians 6:10 says, "Therefore, as we have opportunity, let us do good to all, especially to those who are of the household of faith." God tells us to be good, especially to our children. As we provide for them and bless them, however, we also see that they have a vision for their life, develop self-discipline, and learn teamwork in obtaining the things they want.

## 5.   Find time to work and play with your kids.

Friendships are often developed as you work and play with people, and your kids are no exception. Whether

> >

The key to training up a teenager to love and serve God is to love and serve God yourself. If you are the real deal, then your kids will be the real deal too!

you are doing something out in the yard, working on the car, cleaning the house, or helping a friend move, working with your kids is a great way to get to know them and for them to get to know you in a different setting and situation.

Working with your kids also gives you the opportunity to teach them servanthood and excellence. This is when you fine-tune their attitudes about helping others and doing the best job they can do for those they are helping.

As for playing with your kids, you should have been doing that since they were babies! Parents make the mistake of stopping playing with their kids as they grow older, but kids love it when you just wrestle with them, play games with them, or spontaneously take them to an amusement park to have fun. Again, this is a time when your kids can see you in a different light, when you let down your hair a little and just have a good time with them. And when you're playing games, you also teach them how to play fair while developing their skills in that area.

## Be Mysterious

Did you know that Jesus was a mysterious man in some ways? In fact, seven times in Mark's Gospel it records that people were amazed by the things He did and said. Six times in Matthew's Gospel people *marveled* at Jesus and His works. They were shocked. They didn't expect to hear what they were hearing or see what they were seeing. There was this mystery about Him.

People said things like, "Who is this man Jesus?" "Where did He come from?" and "How can He do and say these things?" I've noticed that certain men and women of God, not just full-time ministers but also business people and athletes and believers in other professions, can have this "mystery" about them too.

What am I talking about? These are people who live and move by the Spirit and the Word, doing great exploits for God. By great exploits, I don't mean raising the dead and stopping a hurricane in its tracks. That's great but not necessarily an everyday occurrence! I'm talking about their vision, wisdom, compassion, and depth of understanding; their ability to meet every challenge and solve difficult problems; and their capacity to love unconditionally.

These are people who cause you to wonder, *How do they do that? How did they stay straight during that trial? Why are they so successful? What gives them the ability to love someone who doesn't deserve anyone's love? How did they know that?*

Kids love to be friends with people who are mysterious in this way. They are drawn to greatness, and every Christian parent has greatness in them. You have the greatness of Jesus Christ inside you, and your teenager wants to see that greatness, that mystery, in you.

There is only one way you can be great, and that is to spend time with the Great One and then live totally for Him. When you spend time with God, He is going to give you secrets. He is going to show you things that you've never seen before. He's going to change your heart and mind to see things the way He sees them, and then you can do things His way.

Most importantly, He's going to tell you things about your kids that you couldn't know any other way. You talk about having your kid's attention! Just walk into their bedroom one day and say, "Son, the Lord just told me that you weren't where you said you were last night. You want to tell me what's going on?"

WOW! That is being Jesus—the friend who sticks closer than a brother—to your teenager. When you walk in the supernatural, amazing, earth-shattering power and wisdom of God, your kids are going to listen when you have something to say to them. They will always wonder what you're thinking and what you're hearing from God! They will know that they can not pull the wool over your eyes when you are partnering with God in the parenting process.

Kids want to be around people who really know God and live by His Word. They want to be friends with those who walk the walk and don't just talk the talk. So we come back to this again. The key to training up a teenager to love and serve God is to love and serve God yourself. If you are the real deal, then your kids will be the real deal too!

# Conclusion>>

I continuously remind myself, "Blaine, you're not the perfect parent and your kids are not going to be perfect kids." And one of the things that encourages me is looking back on when my parents and I got saved. I received Christ and was filled with the Holy Spirit when I was sixteen years old, and my family would follow in the months and years to come, but we still made mistakes. We were trying to figure everything out, and we learned together.

I did some really stupid things those first few years of being born again. I loved Jesus with all my heart, but I still did some things that I am not proud of. But here I am today, serving God in the ministry in a great church. I look at my own kids and think, *Man, my kids are not near as bad as I was, and yet I turned out all right!*

So I encourage you to just keep plugging away at training and preparing your kids for their adult lives. If you live by the Word and are sensitive to God's Spirit, your decisions will be sound, and they're going to be ready when God calls them out of your home and into adulthood. They are going to be ready to make their mark for the Lord Jesus Christ and be mightily blessed of God as they impact their world.

I want to close with a true story that will inspire and motivate you. The first man was Max Jukes. He lived

> >

**What kind of message will you send to the next generation?**

in the eighteenth century in New York and did not believe in Jesus Christ or profess to be a Christian. He refused to take his children to church, even when they asked to go. To date he has had approximately 560 descendants. Of these descendants, 310 died as paupers, 150 were criminals, 7 of them murderers, 100 were known to be alcoholics, and more than half of the women were prostitutes. Most of his descendants made no beneficial contribution to society and cost the U.S. government more than $1.25 million in 19th century dollars.

The second man who lived in the same time period and in the same state was Jonathan Edwards. He was a minister who loved the Lord and saw that his children were in church every Sunday. He has had 1394 descendants. Of these, 295 were college graduates, of whom 13 became university presidents and 65 became professors. Three were elected as United States senators, 3 as state governors. One hundred became lawyers with 1 the dean of a law school, 30 judges, 75 officers in the military, and 100 well-known missionaries, preachers, and authors. Another 80 held public office including 3 mayors of large cities, 1 comptroller of the U.S. Treasury, and 1 vice-president. His family never cost the country one cent, and they have contributed immeasurably to the quality of life in America.[1]

## Conclusion

How is your influence, and what is your legacy? What kind of legacy will you leave with your children? With your grandchildren? With your great-grandchildren? Abraham Lincoln said it like this:

Our children are a timeless message we will send into a generation we will never see.

What kind of message will you send to the next generation? One day, your kids will be parents themselves. It's my hope and prayer that they will be able to look back on how well you raised them and take inspiration and confidence in bringing up their children in the "way they should go" (Prov. 22:6).

# Endnotes>>

## Preface

[1] *The Big Black Book for Parents,* Blaine Bartel, (Tulsa: Harrison House Publishers, 2005), p. 14.

## Chapter 1

[1] *The Big Black Book for Parents,* Blaine Bartel, (Tulsa: Harrison House Publishers, 2005), p. 21.

## Chapter 2

[1] "Why Teenagers Act Weird," Sarah Mahoney, http://www.prevention.com/article/0,5778,s1-6-79-218-3699-1,00.html?

[2] *The Big Black Book for Parents,* Blaine Bartel, (Tulsa: Harrison House Publishers, 2005), p. 3.

## Chapter 3

[1] *Right From Wrong,* Josh McDowell and Bob Hostetler, (Nashville: W. Publishing Group, 1994), p. 156.

[2] *The Big Black Book for Parents,* Blaine Bartel, (Tulsa: Harrison House Publishers, 2005), p. 41.

## Chapter 4

[1] *Webster's New World College Dictionary,* Third Edition, Victoria Neufeldt, Editor-in-Chief (New York: Macmillan, Inc., 1996), p. 18.

[2] *The Big Black Book for Parents,* Blaine Bartel, (Tulsa: Harrison House Publishers, 2005), p. 162.

## Chapter 5

[1] *The Big Black Book for Parents,* Blaine Bartel, (Tulsa: Harrison House Publishers, 2005), p. 4.

## Chapter 6

[1] http:/www.barna.org.

[2] James Strong, *Exhaustive Concordance of the Bible,* "Hebrew and Chaldee Dictionary," (Nashville, TN: Thomas Nelson Publishers, 1984), #3045.

[3] Ibid., #5467.

[4] James Strong, *Exhaustive Concordance of the Bible,* "Hebrew and Chaldee Dictionary," (Nashville, TN: Thomas Nelson Publishers, 1984), #6017, 6014.

[5] *The Big Black Book for Parents,* Blaine Bartel, (Tulsa: Harrison House Publishers, 2005), p. 116.

## Chapter 7

[1] *The Big Black Book for Parents,* Blaine Bartel, (Tulsa: Harrison House Publishers, 2005), p. 51.

## Chapter 8

[1] James Strong, *Exhaustive Concordance of the Bible,* "Greek Dictionary of the New Testament," (Nashville, TN: Thomas Nelson Publishers, 1984), #680, 681.

[2] http://www.heritageymca.org/conference_on_teens.htm.

[3] *The Big Black Book for Parents,* Blaine Bartel (Tulsa: Harrison House Publishers, 2005), p. 99.

## Chapter 9

[1] *Webster's New World College Dictionary,* Third Edition, Victoria Neufeldt, Editor-in-Chief (New York: Macmillan, Inc., 1996), p. 1138, s.v "repent."

[2] *Webster's New World College Dictionary,* Third Edition, Victoria Neufeldt, Editor-in-Chief (New York: Macmillan, Inc., 1996), p. 842, s.v. "mediocre."

[3] Ibid.

[4] *The Big Black Book for Parents,* Blaine Bartel (Tulsa: Harrison House Publishers, 2005), p. 134.

## Chapter 10

[1] A.E. Winship, *Abridgement of Jukes-Edwards,* R.L. Myers & Co., 1900.

## Prayer of Salvation>>

God loves you—no matter who you are, no matter what your past. God loves you so much that He gave His one and only begotten Son for you. The Bible tells us that "…whoever believes in him shall not perish but have eternal life" (John 3:16 NIV). Jesus laid down His life and rose again so that we could spend eternity with Him in heaven and experience His absolute best on earth. If you would like to receive Jesus into your life, say the following prayer out loud and mean it from your heart.

*Heavenly Father, I come to You admitting that I am a sinner. Right now, I choose to turn away from sin, and I ask You to cleanse me of all unrighteousness. I believe that Your Son, Jesus, died on the cross to take away my sins. I also believe that He rose again from the dead so that I might be forgiven of my sins and made righteous through faith in Him. I call upon the name of Jesus Christ to be the Savior and Lord of my life. Jesus, I choose to follow You and ask that You fill me with the power of the Holy Spirit. I declare that right now I am a child of God. I am free from sin and full of the righteousness of God. I am saved in Jesus' name. Amen.*

If you prayed this prayer to receive Jesus Christ as your Savior for the first time, please contact us on the Web at **www.harrisonhouse.com** to receive a free book.

Or you may write to us at:
**Harrison House**
P.O. Box 35035
Tulsa, Oklahoma 74153

# Meet Blaine Bartel>>

**Blaine Bartel** founded Thrive Communications, an organization dedicated to serving those who shape the local church. He is also currently leading a new church launch in a growing area of north Dallas.

Bartel was the founding youth pastor and one of the key strategists in the creation of Oneighty, which has become one of the most emulated youth ministries in the past decade reaching 2,500–3,000 students weekly under his leadership. In a tribute to the long term effects and influence of Blaine's leadership, hundreds of young people that grew up under his ministry are now serving in full time ministry themselves.

A recognized authority on the topics of youth ministry and successful parenting, Bartel is a best-selling author with 12 books published in 4 languages, and is the creator of Thrive—one of the most listened to youth ministry development systems in the country, selling more than 100,000 audio tapes and cd's worldwide. He is one of the most sought after speakers in his field; more than one million people from over 40 countries have attended Blaine Bartel's live seminars or speaking engagements.

His work has been featured in major media including "The Washington Post," cbs' "The Early Show," "The 700 Club," "Seventeen" magazine, as well as newspapers, radio programs, and Internet media worldwide.

Bartel's commitment to creating an enduring legacy that will impact the world is surpassed only by his passion for family as a dedicated father of three children and a loving husband to his wife of more than 20 years, Cathy.

To contact Blaine Bartel,
please write to:

Blaine Bartel
Serving America's Future
P.O. Box 691923
Tulsa, OK 74169


Or visit him on his Web site at:
www.blainebartel.com

## Take the Turn for God in Just
## 5 Minutes a Day>>

Witty, short, and inspiring devotions for teens from one of America's youth leadership specialists!

Teens can discover a real, action-packed, enthusiastic relationship with God. The *thrive.teen.devotional* is motivated by a very simple challenge: Give just five minutes a day to God and watch your life turn around.

At the end of eight weeks, the Word of God is going to be more real and alive to teens than ever before as they gain spiritual insights on issues like friendships, self-esteem, and prayer. The good news is that when one's mind is renewed, they experience a radical turn-around in every other area of their life, too.

thrive.teen.devotional
by Blaine Bartel
1-57794-777-0

# Other Books by Blaine Bartel>>

every teenager's
**little black book**
on reaching your dreams

every teenager's
**little black book**
of God's guarantees

every teenager's
**little black book**
on how to get along with your parents

every teenager's
**little black book**
for athletes

every teenager's
**little black book**
on how to win a friend to Christ

every teenager's
**little black book**
on sex and dating

every teenager's
**little black book**
on cash

every teenager's
**little black book**
on cool

every teenager's
**little black book**
of hard to find information

every teenager's
**little black book**
for graduates

for more information on the *little black book* series,
please visit our web site at:
**www.littleblackbooks.info**

# www.harrisonhouse.com

## *Fast. Easy. Convenient!*

- ◆ New Book Information
- ◆ Look Inside the Book
- ◆ Press Releases
- ◆ Bestsellers
- ◆ Free E-News
- ◆ Author Biographies

- ◆ Upcoming Books
- ◆ Share Your Testimony
- ◆ Online Product Availability
- ◆ Product Specials
- ◆ Order Online

For the latest in book news and author information, please visit us on the Web at www.harrisonhouse.com. Get up-to-date pictures and details on all our powerful and life-changing products. Sign up for our e-mail newsletter, *Friends of the House,* and receive free monthly information on our authors and products including testimonials, author announcements, and more!

Harrison House—
*Books That Bring Hope, Books That Bring Change*

## The Harrison House Vision>>

Proclaiming the truth and the power
Of the Gospel of Jesus Christ
With excellence;

Challenging Christians to
Live victoriously,
Grow spiritually,
Know God intimately.